The Burning Forest is an anthology of modern Polish poets, from Norwid to Bronisław Maj, translated by one of the world's leading Polish translators and featuring large selections of poems, biographies and photographs. It includes major poets such as Herbert, Różewicz and Szymborska, wartime writer-heroes like Stroiński, and young dissidents who have made their mark during the past ten years.

The book begins with Norwid (1821-1883), the great post-romantic poet, at first abused and neglected, but eventually recognised as the guiding spirit of modern Polish poetry. It then focuses on poetry written since the outbreak of the Second World War, including the late work of Leopold Staff, work by poets involved in the wartime resistance (Stroiński, Różewicz), poets who began to flourish after the demise of Stalinism (Herbert, Karpowicz, Woroszylski, Szymborska, Bursa), exiles (Darowski, Czaykowski, Czerniawski) and the new wave poets (Krynicki, Barańczak, Kowalska, Maj).

All anthologies provoke controversies over which writers they include or exclude. This book will be no exception, for Adam Czerniawski's selection is based not just on the established Polish canon but on a stipulation that to merit inclusion a translation must stand up as a poem in English. His choices are also personal: these are the poets he has translated over the years, the poets he has wanted to translate for English readers.

The cover shows a detail from Forest Fire *by Piero di Cosimo (Ashmolean Museum, Oxford).*

The Burning Forest

translated and edited by

ADAM CZERNIAWSKI

BLOODAXE BOOKS

Copyright © Adam Czerniawski 1979, 1982, 1983, 1988

ISBN: 1 85224 009 1

First published 1988 by
Bloodaxe Books Ltd,
P.O. Box 1SN,
Newcastle upon Tyne NE99 1SN.

Bloodaxe Books Ltd acknowledges
the financial assistance of Northern Arts.

Typesetting by Bryan Williamson, Manchester.

Cover printing by
Tyneside Free Press Workshop Ltd, Newcastle upon Tyne.

Printed in Great Britain by
Bell & Bain Limited, Glasgow, Scotland.

No time to mourn roses, when forests burn
JULIUSZ SŁOWACKI

Acknowledgements

The translations of poems by Tadeusz Różewicz are taken from *Conversation with the Prince and other poems* (Anvil Press Poetry, 1982), those by Leopold Staff from *An Empty Room* (Bloodaxe Books, 1983), and those by Leon Zdzisław Stroiński from *Window* (Oasis Books, 1979).

Some of the translations have previously appeared in *Encounter, The Guardian, Index on Censorship, Modern Poetry in Translation, New Statesman, The New Review, Oficyna Poetów, PN Review, Poetry Wales, Prism International, Shearsman* and *Stand*, and some were included in *A Matter of Taste* (BBC Radio 3).

Thanks are due to Michael March for seeking out the photographs of Zbigniew Herbert, Ryszard Krynicki and Wiktor Woroszylski.

The photographs are by Piotr Czaykowski (Czaykowski), Joanna Helander (Krynicki), Ella van der Hulst (Różewicz), Danuta B. Łomaczewska (Staff and Szymborska), Ingeborg Lommatzsch (Woroszylski), Tomasz Michalak (Kowalska), Jerzy Siracki (Karpowicz) and A. Sulik (Barańczak). The drawing of Adam Czerniawski is by Feliks Topolski.

Contents

ZBIGNIEW HERBERT (born 1924)

JAN DAROWSKI (born 1926)

WIKTOR WOROSZYLSKI (born 1927)

ANDRZEJ BURSA (1932-1957)

Some explanation is required of the long delay which attended the publication of this volume.

I had reason to hope that I should have obtained the active co-operation and assistance of several Polish friends, interested in the literary reputation of their country, – but communication is so difficult, and on certain subjects so dangerous, that I have been disappointed; and have felt myself compelled to decide on now ushering these imperfect Specimens into the world, rather than indulge a longer hesitation, which would have led probably to the total abandonment of my purpose. My determination would have been different, had I seen any chance that abler hands would fill the chasm in foreign literature, which an almost total ignorance of Polish authors has left. All that I can now hope for is, to prepare the way for some future and more intelligent student: – and all that I can promise is, to go on collecting materials, in order to supply hereafter the deficiencies of the present work.

JOHN BOWRING,
Specimens of the Polish Poets
(London, 1827)

INTRODUCTION

This anthology represents some of the poets who were born between the end of World War I and the end of World War II, and whose work covers the period from World War II to the present. But it opens with selections from two contrasting father-figures: Cyprian Norwid (1821-1883), who is the patron saint of modernism in 20th century Polish poetry; and Leopold Staff (1878-1957), whose carefully crafted poetry spans the whole of the first half of this century. Staff responded to new poetic currents released during World War II, and this combination of conservatism and adaptability earned him special respect among younger poets after the War.

The Poles are touchingly old-fashioned and sentimental: in the second half of the 20th century they still believe in the value and effectiveness of poetry. Their trust has its roots in the early 19th century when the country's political collapse coincided with an unprecedented flowering of poetic talent. The intense nationalism of Adam Mickiewicz (1798-1855), Juliusz Słowacki (1809-1849) and Zygmunt Krasiński (1812-1859), coupled with their intransigent conviction, eloquently voiced in their poetry, persuaded millions that in the end the national spirit will prevail against temporal oppression.

When Mickiewicz was born, Poland had already ceased to exist. As a student, he was involved in conspiratorial work which earned him several years' deportation to Russia. He subsequently lived in exile in Western Europe, dividing his time between writing and political activism. He died of cholera in Istanbul, trying to raise a Polish liberation army, having abandoned poetry some years previously. The pattern was set for the classic Polish dilemma: is not a life of contemplation, at a time when the nation faces a crisis, a self-indulgence that is morally reprehensible? Not that Mickiewicz was an escapist writer – in his major work *Forefathers' Eve* he portrays with agonising vividness the persecution of Wilno University students by Tsarist authorities.

While *Forefathers' Eve* is a tribute to Polish heroism and suffering, his *Konrad Wallenrod* teaches the lesson of stealth, deception and simulated collaborationism with the occupying force, and *Pan Tadeusz*, a narrative poem of Polish country life at the turn of the century, ends with the arrival of Napoleon's army of liberation in 1812. Of the retreat from Moscow there is only a hint. Thus Mickiewicz offers his countrymen three incompatible lessons: desperate heroism, cunning or self-delusion. Curiously, what in the end helped the nation to survive as an entity for over a century, despite being partitioned into constituent provinces of three neighbouring empires, was in fact self-delusion. Rationally, there was no hope for the re-emergence of an independent Polish state. It was the poets living in exile who greatly helped to sustain the nation's awareness of its identity when in a formal sense there was no identity left. There is a profound and characteristically Polish irony in a situation whereby a leading poet abandons poetry in favour of direct action, fails completely, and in the end contributes to the nation's survival precisely through his rejected creative work.

Born in 1821, Cyprian Norwid also spent most of his life in exile. He knew the great Romantic poets and Chopin in the West as older, now famous colleagues. He himself was not to achieve any significant recognition. His increasingly laconic verse, with its crabbed syntax and daring imagery, proved too much for a readership which had now grown complacently accustomed to the seductive simplicities of Mickiewicz's ballads, love sonnets and epic evocations of hunting, feasting and brawling in rural Lithuania. Norwid, a difficult, eccentric man, no doubt helped to ensure that his writings should be largely ignored or ridiculed during his lifetime and forgotten after his death in 1883 until they were rescued from oblivion at the turn of the century by Zenon Przesmycki.

Norwid said in a letter that 'a perfect lyric should be like a plaster cast: those boundaries where forms miss each other and leave cracks ought to be preserved and not smoothed over with a knife...What Poles call lyrics are but chopped meat and mazurkas.' Characteristically, the example he used to illustrate the thought is drawn not from literature but from sculpture. This advocate and practitioner of incomplete statements and enigmatic silences was also an accomplished graphic artist and sculptor, but paradoxically a life-long champion of Wincklemann's neoclassicism and its embodiment in the smooth, totally unenigmatic and fully rounded work of Canova and Ary Scheffer. For a man who spent decades in and around Paris in those crucial years, he shows amazingly little interest in the non-academic art of the time. There is only the oracular and puzzling polemical piece 'Citizen Gustave Courbet' in which Norwid expresses a very guarded approval of the artist. The only other contemporary artist of any consequence whom he ever mentions is Puvis de Chavannes. The poet who is now recognised as the precursor of modern Polish poetry was in many respects traditionalist and conservative. Interestingly, a similar conflict may be observed in many representatives of 20th century avant-garde. Perhaps this contradiction is not, after all, so strange: political radicalism demands total centralised control of the population and therefore harnesses every means, including art, to achieve this end. Inevitably, the art in question must be popular in appeal: it cannot risk being experimental, and therefore "obscure", with its consequent limited appeal to a potentially hostile clique and in danger of provoking governmental hostility on the suspicion that the breaking of artistic norms may encourage readers to question stable aspects of social and political order.

Norwid has been compared with Gerard Manley Hopkins.* The analogy seems irresistible: two contemporaries persevering in total isolation to renovate the language, rhythms, imagery and structure of poetry, and triumphing only after death. Both Catholics; both sensitive idealists horrified by the brutalities of rampant industrialisation; both also accomplished practitioners of art and endowed with a deep understanding and love of music; both ascetics partly through choice, partly through necessity, the one in holy orders, the other never far from them; both displaying passionate sensuality and sublimated eroticism in their poetry. And yet, reading Hopkins one is never struck by the thought 'This could have been written by Norwid', or *vice versa*. But why should we expect this kind of affinity? Hopkins had never read Norwid and Norwid had never read Hopkins. Moreover, both were highly idiosyncratic experimenters in very different languages. But the same is true of Emily Dickinson, and yet, when reading some of her lyrics, one has the uncanny feeling that one is reading English-language equivalents of Norwid's poems. Thus Dickinson's:

> Not one of all the purple host
> Who took the flag today
> Can tell the definition
> So clear of victory
> As when defeated, dying,
> On whose forbidden ear
> The distant strains of triumph
> Burst agonised and clear.

is equivalent in tone, style and imagery to Norwid's 'Out of harmony' (below, p.35). What is no less remarkable is the fact that the two poems were composed by such different people in very different historical circumstances. In Dickinson's poetry we have the spiritual turmoils of a provincial spinsterish recluse, in Norwid's an acute awareness of contemporary social and political upheavals, and

---

* E.g. cf. J. Peterkiewicz, 'Introducing Norwid', *Slavonic and East European Review*, 27, no.68 (December 1948), 228-47.

especially of the Polish predilection for hasty, ill-judged insurrec-
tions against ruthless occupying powers. 'Out of harmony' is a cry
of political dissent clothed in biblical imagery, while some of his
aphorisms explicitly condemn the Poles' inability to think through
the human costs of political activism.

Norwid's chiselled lyrical miniatures, which nevertheless are
unclassically mysterious, have an affinity with the formal purity of
Gautier's poems, and these, we know, served as a lesson in craft for
the author of 'Mauberley' and the author of the Prufrock quatrains.
The cadences, the thematic organisation and juxtapositions of the
Pound and Eliot poems, are strikingly similar to those of Norwid's
poems, down to the explicit evocations of Greek myths of sexual
encounters. Compare Pound's

> 'Daphne with her thighs in bark
> Stretches toward me her leafy hands' –
> Subjectively. In the stuffed-satin drawing-room
> I await The Lady Valentine's commands,
>
> Knowing my coat has never been
> Of precisely the fashion
> To stimulate, in her,
> a durable passion...

with Eliot's

> Morning stirs the feet and hands
>   (Nausicaa and Polypheme).
> Gesture of orang-outang
>   Rises from the sheets in steam.
>   . . .
> Sweeney addressed full length to shave
>   Broadbottomed, pink from nape to base,
> Knows the female temperament
>   And wipes the suds around his face.

and with Norwid's 'Nerves', and his ballad 'Undressed'.* It is hard
to believe that 'Undressed', a powerful, concise poem ending with

---

* The sordid world of Sweeney has of course nothing in common with the
refinements of elegant drawing-rooms, but the technique of violently jux-
taposing incompatible cultures is shared by the three poets. Admittedly,
'Nerves' makes no reference to classical myth, but it contains instead the
Christian symbol of the Cross which plays a similar role of counterpointing
two very different worlds. Moreover, the similarity between Norwid's and
Pound's evocations of the drawing-room is in itself remarkable enough to
merit attention.

a terse account of the celebrated ancient myth of voyeurism and violence:

> Caught in brightness, Actaeon blenched;
>   The hounds ignore the trumpets' din,
> The Hyperborean Wood stands terror-struck
>   Quivering like a threadbare shack.

is in fact a parable of the partition of Poland (!). If this is so, we learn something important both about Polish nationalism and about Norwid's frustrated sexuality.* He hopelessly pursued across Europe the renowned beauty Maria Kalergis, and his other infatuations probably also remained unconsummated.

Despite formal, though spasmodic education in art, intellectually Norwid was self-taught, which accounts for the crankiness of some of his ideas, especially those grandiose historiosophical speculations based on a do-it-yourself philology, though this method anticipates the practices of the far from self-taught Martin Heidegger. This alienated him even more from his contemporaries, who had neither the patience nor the intelligence to glean his insights and appreciate his single-minded pursuit of the highest artistic standards.

In 1939 Poland went to war imbued with the romantic spirit of Mickiewicz who had urged readers of his 'Ode to youth' to pitch their efforts according to their lofty aims. Just as the Polish spirit, sustained by the nation's cultural heritage, remained unbroken throughout the 19th century, so an effort of will would triumph over Nazi armour. The trauma of defeat, yet another partition of the country between Russians and Germans, the bestiality of both occupying powers, finally called into question the idealism which had dominated Polish thinking for the previous hundred years. Perhaps the model should be not the fearless students of Mickiewicz's *Forefathers' Eve* but rather the cunning Konrad Wallenrod, or even Mickiewicz himself finally despairing of the value of literature.

This last conclusion was the one reached by Czesław Miłosz and Tadeusz Różewicz, both of whom had experienced the German occupation. Miłosz argued that 'art is not an equal partner with

---

* I say 'is in fact a parable of the partition of Poland' because this is the interpretation offered by the distinguished Norwid scholar Juliusz Gomulicki based on apparently irrefutable historico-literary evidence. However, I argue strongly (in *Prochy i pyłki, Archipelag*, April 1986, West Berlin) against the view that the poem is a riddle with a political message, claiming that we must accept the work's overt sexual theme on its face value.

historical events. Famine and death are more powerfully expressive
than the most inspired poetic stanza or the most beautifully painted
picture.' He was questioning the value of all art, asking

> What is poetry which does not save
> Nations or people?
> A connivance with official lies

The reply in poetry's defence was provided some thirty years later
by Ryszard Krynicki, who is especially persuasive since no one could
possibly accuse this resolute dissident of conniving with any official
lies:

> What is poetry, which obviously
> saves neither nations nor people,
> nor nations from people,
> nor people from nations,
> nor nations and people
> from themselves?
> What is poetry, which saves
> that which nations and people
> so easily destroy?

Różewicz was affected by the war in a remarkably similar way.
He too began by trusting literature: 'I searched books and poems
for practical help. I hoped they would help me overcome despair
and doubt...And when this led to disappointment – after all these
were only books – I became angry and disillusioned with the greatest
works.' Różewicz's coming of age as a poet coincided with the end
of the war and he saw his task primarily as one of rebuilding, against
all odds, human trust in the world. Such poetry had to be puritanically
stark, completely free from ornamental prettiness. After the holo-
caust, the poet, like Adam in the Garden of Eden, has to construct
a world by simply naming objects:

> After the end of the world
> after death
> I found myself in the midst of life
> creating myself
> building life
> people animals landscapes
>
> this is a table I said
> this is a table
> there is bread and a knife on the table

It is noteworthy that neither Miłosz nor Różewicz had taken their
own conclusions seriously: they have continued to write copiously

and have attempted to justify this self-contradiction by treating poetry as, according to Miłosz, 'a kind of higher politics, an unpolitical politics'. There is here the danger of turning poetry into a running political commentary. Many poets have accepted this role (the temptation to be acknowledged as the conscience of the nation is very alluring) but Zbigniew Herbert distinctly has not and many of his poems possess a specific significance and resonance precisely because he has the artistic sensitivity which enables him to judge how far he can go without compromising himself as a poet. In his justly celebrated 'Fortinbras elegising' Herbert demonstrates that the reflective Hamlet cannot also be the briskly political Fortinbras. He enunciates this message directly in the interview quoted below (pages 106-107) in his biographical note.

The one poet who always well understood the position adopted by Herbert is Staff. His tacit adherence to this programme throughout his life seems even more remarkable after his endurance of Nazi occupation in Warsaw and the ruthless pressures of Stalinist social-realism, both periods coinciding with the production of his most impressive work. His response to the inspirers of controlled literature is stated obliquely with characteristic self-deprecating irony in 'A song' (p.47 below) and in the following significantly entitled 'Grand ode to the stars':

> Be not ashamed of glory, stars,
> Let ironic voices mock:
> The universe is as splendid
> As a factory chimney-stack.

The dangers and the illusory benefits of *voluntary* political and moral commitment are summarised in Norwid's preface to his *Vademecum* sequence composed in 1865:

> In a word, I think we shall pass on to a new Epoch and – dare I say – a *more normal one*; for poetry, *as a force*, survives all manner of temporal conditions, but it does not equally survive them *as an art*. Indeed, it gains *power* to the extent that it takes over the activities of others, close to it, who neglect to do their job. But in this gaining of *power*, it loses its *art*. This then is the present state of Polish poetry and its duo-polarity causes it to find itself at a critical point.

Norwid's analysis continues to be relevant because the pressures upon Polish poetry have not changed either in their severity or their nature. The 'normal epoch' has still not dawned and is unlikely to in the foreseeable future.

Any anthology of translated poetry is always distorted by having to
exclude the untranslatable, and the untranslatable is often the best,
or even, some say, is always the best. Is it a coincidence that
Kochanowski, Mickiewicz, Słowacki and Leśmian remain practically
unknown to English-speaking readers? But then, until some 25 years
ago, this was true of *all* Polish poetry, yet since then many Polish
poets have been published in anthologies and individual volumes in
Britain, USA and Canada. They all happen to be 20th century poets.
And this fact leads to the observation that the pre-modern poets
(specifically those in the Romantic tradition, which of course
includes Mickiewicz and Słowacki, but also projects well into the
20th century) translate badly because they operate in a highly rhetor-
ical mode which it is very difficult to render credible in English. It
is therefore no accident that this anthology opens with Norwid, who
gradually frees himself from the massive dominance of Mickiewicz
and Słowacki and evolves a poetic language which is harsh and
elliptical; that it continues with post-war Staff who in his late poetry
turns his back on his own exulting and exalted pre-war compositions;
and that finally it focuses on poets who in various ways have tried
to evolve a "naked" style (Różewicz, Bursa), or have relied on the
quiet subtleties of Norwidian irony (Herbert) or have composed
open declarative verse (Krynicki, Barańczak) modelled to some
extent on e.e. cummings, Brecht and the Beat poets.

   Another reason for the impenetrability by foreigners of those
Polish works which have made the strongest impact on Polish con-
sciousness is less to do with the formal difficulties of those works
than with their hermetically Polish-centred content. It is a common
feature of the poems included here that they either place their Polish-
ness in a wider context or avoid it altogether. Herbert in particular
has succeeded in universalising the ordeals of his generation by
embedding them in the wider cultural and political history of the
West. Różewicz has similarly generalised the experiences of Nazi
occupation and post-war attempts to rebuilt normality. He has
achieved this via an arresting immediacy of expression which
required nothing less than a revolution in poetic language.

   So, if this anthology is circumscribed by what one particular trans-
lator has found it possible to translate, this should not be seen as a
wholly negative principle of selection. What needs stressing is not
so much that I have been discarding the untranslatable, as that I
have been seeking out the translatable. In this search for the trans-
latable I became convinced that I was simply looking for good poems.
It gradually became clear to me that translatability is a strong indi-
cator of merit: in order to be able to translate one needs to discover

in the original a kernel of meaning, and if there is no discernible meaning, there is nothing there to translate.

Organicists will here protest at this search for essences of paraphrasable meanings: what we are supposed to be translating is the total linguistic experience, and given poetry's reliance on metaphor and the specific qualities of a particular language, it is not surprising that the best poetry is pretty well untranslatable.

The argument has some force, but it must accept the consequence: good poetry is untranslatable because it is meaningless. On the other hand, the case for translatability, while possibly prone to the paraphrasable meanings heresy, does not depend on it. It assumes meaning to be pervasive in poetic use of language and also accepts that some poets work hard to obscure it. It is the fact that in the poets here represented meaning is paramount that they have proved satisfying to translate.

Bogdan Czaykowski, who has given me valuable advice on the Norwid translations, complains that in general I have 'interpreted' Norwid, thus depriving him of ambiguities and subtleties of meaning – and of obscurities – which the reader ought to have the satisfaction of unravelling for himself.

This may in effect be an aspect of the untranslatability of poetry thesis or an application of a judgment – expressed in a different context by a character in a Norwid short-story – that 'Redaction means Reduction'. But if my thesis about the semantic kernels in poems is correct, then *a* meaning has to be teased out of the original before a translation can be attempted. But what then of the other layers of meaning and penumbras of meaning allegedly ignored? My answer rests on an assumption that natural languages are all inherently polysemic and that therefore the extraction of a single meaning is not equivalent to a construction of sentences of formal logic. The natural language of the translation has its own polysemic parameters which the translator can rely on to render the translation rich in meaning. Significantly, logicians are plagued by ambiguities when they try to decode a formal sequence into a natural language. Notoriously, these polysemic parameters are different in different languages and hence the familiar problems with synonyms, homonyms, puns, *double-entendres*, proverbs and idioms, never mind the deliberately engineered poetic ambiguities. It is therefore futile and often counter-productive to try to carry over in translation the full semantic variety of the original. It may be more effective to isolate one semantic layer and let the language of the translation exert its own magic.

If this view of translation leaves out people like Słowacki, Leśmian

and Przyboś, this is not because their poems are necessarily a mean-
ingless verbiage but because the meanings they have are so reliant
on the genius of the Polish language that what is required is not so
much translation as recreation in another language, the translator
allowing himself to be led by that new language's specific and unique
possibilities regarding synonymy, homonymy, word-association and
word-sounds.

The debate will doubtless continue. Meanwhile, I hope that the
translations that follow are sufficiently creative to convey some
notion of their originals.

ADAM CZERNIAWSKI

Cyprian Kamil Norwid was born in 1821 in Laskowo-Głuchy near Warsaw and died in Paris in 1883. His parents died when he was a child and he was brought up by his grandmother. He attended grammar school in Warsaw and later worked in the College of Arms there and also studied painting.

Norwid left Poland in 1842 on a tour of Germany and Italy. The Tsarist government in partitioned Poland was pressing for his return and when he was in Berlin in 1846 persuaded the Prussian authorities to arrest him. He was however released after some months and made his way to Rome where in 1848 Adam Mickiewicz was organising the Polish Legion to liberate Poland, but eventually Norwid decided not to enroll.

In 1849 Norwid left Rome, making his way indirectly to Paris where he stayed until 1852. He then departed to New York via London, whence he returned via Liverpool and London to Paris in 1854. He stayed in Paris for the rest of his life.

'When I was a clerk at the Polish College of Arms, I spent more of my time in the office reading than working, and I used to go mainly in order that my grandfather of blessed memory, colonel Michał Sobieski, who was the State Counsellor there, should see me at my desk. For he had hopes of my becoming a "decent man" – but he was disappointed!'

'Prose-writer, critic, poet, sculptor, painter, he daily demonstrates immense fruitfulness and creativity.' (*Przegląd Poznański*, 1848)

'A mannered obscurity of thought, imagery and language.' (*Gazeta Polska*, 1849)

'I do not defend myself against the accusation that I am obscure *in my writings – an accusation which does not invite communication but rather rejects finally – for in what language can someone whose language is impossible to understand explain himself?'*

'...it is very difficult to grasp these poems, logically tie the author's thoughts and say what he is after.' (*Czas*, 1851)

'There are those who teach that poetry needs subjects which are not dry and graceless. A poetry which in order to be poetry requires non-dry subjects and awaits graceful ones lies outside my competence.'

'I am in London: Drummond Street (Euston Square) Hotel Nelson. Don't tell anyone and don't recommend me to any Poles, whom en masse, *God knows, I love dearly, but individually they have done me too much harm.'*
[1854]

'...I lived there [in London] in almost the poorest house in the poorest district of the city.'

'Deaf and destitute, Cyprian ekes out his life in New York...' (Lanckoroński, 1854)

'A veritable ruin of what was there once: the old pride, the old self-confidence erased by misfortunes and battles... When I started reminiscing about Warsaw...tears came into our eyes!' (Józef Dziekoński, 1856)

'Examples of studied nothingness, in which quirks of thought are matched by quirks of language and unbelievable arrogance competes with glaring ignorance.' (Wiadomości Polskie, 1857)

'He is a wretched ruin, the sadder since there never was a finished edifice.' (Andrzej Koźmian, 1859)

'Loneliness – loneliness – loneliness.' [1860]

'Monsieur,
    J'ai reçu votre aimable lettre, dans laquelle vous me faites des éloges pour la protection que j'ai été à même de donner aux pauvres chrétiens de cette ville. Votre charmante poésie, que vous m'avez adressée à cette même occasion, m'est aussi parvenue...' (Abd el Kader, Damascus, 1860)

'Wagner's Tannhaüser... has been called the music of the future, just as our people call Norwid the poet of the future, and indeed it is a Norwidian work: Hegelian philosophy in music.' (Andrzej Koźmian, 1861)

'When my Vade mecum appears in print they will then see and realise what is a proper lyric in the Polish language, for they as yet have not had any acquaintance with it and have not got the slightest idea of it.' [1867]

'A cigarette in his lips, he discussed art with the enthusiasm and faith of youth, which neither age nor life's vicissitudes managed to dim. Colourful words and beautiful thoughts flowed from the lips of a sick man.' (Pantaleon Szyndler, 1876)

'Extremely individualistic and precisely because of this individualism there is no way he can be well understood by the masses.' (Echo, 1877)

'In the capital of excess and vitality, on the outskirts of Paris pulsating with life, lonely and poor, he is like a monument to the past...he resembles an Indian fakir...' (Przegląd Tygodniowy, 1879)

'ACTE DE DÉCÈS de Cyprien Norwid, âgé de cinquante cinq ans, peintre, né à Varsovie (Pologne), décédé en son domicile rue du Chevaleret 119, ce matin à sept heures...DRESSÉ...sur la déclaration de Michel Zaleski.'

Although witnessed by a loyal friend, the certificate misstates Norwid's age and place of birth and describes him as a painter rather than poet. Always sensitive to the ironies of fate, Norwid would have relished this one too.

'Cyprian Norwid is dead. So ?...Cyprian's truly beautiful poems could make up a volume which would prove its weight even alongside the best European talents but will there be anyone to offer him this posthumous favour?' (Teofil Lenartowicz, 1883)

'Poor poet-painter! Has left no distinct heritage.' (Konstancja Morawska, 1886)

'Norwid's works demand not just to be read, but to be closely read.' (Wiktor Gomulicki, 1902)

'Today, even after the publication of just a handful of unknown works, his name sounds...just as fully...as the names of our three great Romantics.' (Zenon Przesmycki, first editor of Norwid's works, 1904)

'[Norwid's manuscripts] might just as well and with no injury to the poet have remained hidden.' (Piotr Chmielowski, leading literary historian, 1904)

Collected Works published 1971-76 by Juliusz Gomulicki, son of Wiktor Gomulicki.

A funeral rhapsody in memory of General Bem*

'Iusiurandum patri datum usque ad hanc diem *ita servavi...'*
                                                        HANNIBAL

I
– Why ride away, Shadow, hands broken on the mail,
Sparks of torches playing around your knees – ?
The laurel-green sword is spattered with candle tears,
The falcon strains, your horse jerks its foot like a dancer.
– Pennons in the wind blow against each other
Like moving tents of nomad armies in the sky.
Long trumpets shake sobbing and banners
Bow their wings which droop from above
Like spear-pierced dragons, lizards and birds...
Like the many ideas you caught with your spear...

II
– Mourning maidens go, some lifting their arms
Filled with scent-sheaves torn apart by the wind;
Some gather into shells tears breaking from the cheek,
Some still seek the road that *was built centuries ago...*
Others dash against the ground huge pots of clay
Whose clatter in cracking yet adds to the sorrow.

III
– Boys strike hatchets blue against the sky,
Serving lads strike light-rusted shields,
A mighty banner sways amid the smoke, its spear-point
Leaning, as it were, against the arcs of heaven...

IV
They enter and drown in the valley...emerge in the moonlight
Blackening the sky, an icy glare brushes them
And glimmers on blades of spears like a star unable to fall,
The chant suddenly ceased, then splashed out like a wave...

V
On – on – till it's time to roll into the grave:
We shall behold a black chasm lurking beyond the road
(And to cross it humanity will not find a way)
Over the edge we shall spear-thrust your steed
As though with a rusting spur...

VI
And we'll drag the procession, saddening *slumber-seized cities*,
Battering gates with urns, whistling on blunted hatchets,
Till the walls of Jericho tumble down like logs,
Swooned hearts revive – nations gather the must from their eyes...

. . . .
On – on – –

[1851]

* General Józef Bem (1794-1850) commanded Polish and Hungarian
revolutionary armies during the 1848 nationalist revolts. A convert to Islam,
he died in Aleppo in Syria. [Ed.]

On board the 'Margaret Evans' sailing this day to New-York
London, December, 1852, 10 am

I
Occasional sun squibs glisten on sails,
Brush the masts and splash on waves;
Mists disappear like a *woman's veil*,
Behind it rise *ruin-like* clouds!..

II
'Why ruins ? And why a veil ?
Why a woman's... ?' Let the critic demand,
Let him blame the Muse for the muddled
Concepts in her mind –

III
I don't know...I see and sketch this sadly
As though I were one of the flying cranes
That drag their shadow across the sails
Not thinking whether any trace remains...

IV

I don't know...the end, perhaps I never do,
But...

> (here the helmsman cried)

– Adieu !

To Emir Abd el Kader in Damascus

Praise of living virtuous men
Is like praising God himself,
And good news received with love
Is like the Ghost in Mary's womb.

Accept then, Sir, a distant tribute,
You, who are like a shield of God;
May an orphan's tears, a cripple's tears
Shine as baptism on your head.

The one God reigns from age to age,
None knows the measure of His favours;
He bids the nails drop from his wounds,
He orders stars to shine as spurs;

His foot is in the rainbow's stirrup,
He rides to Judgement day;
Who gave Him earth and sky?
Who gave Him light and shade?

And if in tears of tortured men,
If in innocent maidens' blood,
If in the waking child,
There is only the one God,

Then let your tent be broader
Than David's cedar groves;
For of the Magi you were first
To mount your horse upon the hour!

[1860]

Yesterday – and – I

A deafness sad and rare
When you hear
The Word, but miss
The accent and stress.

For an angel calls...But they mock:
'Thunder!'
So you slam the coffin lid over your face under
The rock.

You have no wish to cry
'Eloi...Eloi' – why ?
– Ah, God, sails lap the northern gale,
Seas rail.

A hum in my ear (I have no theory
Regarding storms)
So I dream and feel a folio of history
Turn to stone...

[26 December 1860]

My Country

Those who say my country means
Meadows, flowers and fields of wheat,
Hamlets and trenches, must confess
                    These are her feet.

The child is not forced from his mother's arms,
The youth at her side will grow
While she leans on her eldest son,
                    These are my laws.

My country's brow has not risen here;
My flesh's beyond Euphrates and the Flood,
My spirit soars above Chaos,
                    I pay rent to the world.

No nation fashioned or saved me,
I recall eternity's span;
David's key unlocked my lips,
                    Rome called me man.

I fall on the sand to wipe with my hair
My country's blood-stained feet,
But I know her face and crown
                    Radiant like the sun of suns.

My ancestors have known no other;
Her feet with my hand I used to feel;
I often kissed the clumsy sandal strap
                    Round her heel.

They needn't teach me where my country lies;
Hamlets, trenches and fields of wheat,
Flesh and blood and this her scar
                    Are her print, her feet.

[Paris, January 1861]

Marionettes

1
Wouldn't you be bored when a million
Silent stars shine around the world,
Each cluster sparkling in a different mould,
All still – yet flying ?

2
Still the earth, the aeons vast,
And those living at this hour
Of whom not a bone will last,
Though men will be as now.

3
Wouldn't you be bored on a stage
So amateurish and small,
Where everyone's Ideals rage
And the show is paid with life?

4
Truly, how is one to kill time,
I am most sincerely bored;
What remedy, Madam, should I explore,
Shall I write prose or rhyme?

5
Or write nothing…just sit in the sun
Absorbed in that fine romance
Composed by the Flood upon grains of sand,
Doubtless for the amusement of man – (!)

6
Or better still – I know a braver way
Against this damned *ennui*:
Forget *people*, make calls on *persons*,
Wear a neatly fashioned tie!…

[1861]

Generalities

When like a butterfly the Artist spirit
In spring of life inhales the air,
It can but say:
'*The earth is round – it is a sphere.*'

But when autumnal shivers
Shake the trees and kill the flowers,
It must elaborate:
'*Though somewhat flattened at the poles.*'

Amid the varied charms
Of eloquence and Rhyme
One persists above the rest:
    *   *   *   *   *   *
A proper word each thing to name!

The past

The *past*, death and pain are not acts of God,
But of law-breaking man,
Who therefore lives in dread
And sensing evil, wants *oblivion*.

But is he not like a child in a dray
Crying, 'Oh, look, the oak's
Disappearing in the wood…',
While the oak's still and the child's borne away?

The past is now – though somewhat far:
Behind the dray a village barn,
And not *something somewhere*
Never seen by man!…

In Verona

Above the house of Capulet and Montague,
Thunder-moved, washed in dew,
Heaven's gentle eye

Looks on ruins of hostile city-states,
On broken garden gates,
And drops a star from on high.

It is for Juliet, a cypress whispers,
For Romeo that tear
Seeps through the tomb.

But men say knowingly and mock
It was not a tear but a rock
Awaited by none.

Narcissus

1
Narcissus, reflecting a satisfied face,
Cried, 'Let everyone note:
As I am supreme, so is Greece.'
Thereupon Echo spoke,

2
'These nymph haunts, this lake,
And the depths of sapphire slopes
Are not solely from your Greece,
But – from light, clouds and mists...'

3
'Your shape, note, how shimmering,
Though you gaze in a crystal pool –
Reflection comes from the distant *sun*,
Only the deep is your constant *home*.'

Out of harmony

Round God's manger
The chosen few are singing;
But at the door
Others catch their breath...

And what of those
Now entering the town
Where the ear still rings
With *innocents' cries!*...

Sing you who are chosen
There where He was born;
My ear is pierced
By the pursuing horn...

Sing in triumphant chorus
Your praises unto God –
I could spoil your song:
I have seen *blood!*...

Mysticism

1

A mystic ? He's wrong – for sure!
Is there no mystic way?
It's a melancholy void,
A dream – till break of day!...

2

Does a highlander,
Lost in cloud and rain,
Doubt the cloud's there
    *   *   *   *   *   *
When lost – again?

Tenderness

Tenderness – is like a cry full of war;
And like the current of whispering springs,
And like a funeral march...

And like a long plait of golden hair
On which a widower wears
A silver watch – – –

Gods and man

1
Today authors are like God:
They breathe and a masterpiece is born,
The heavy plough soars in wingèd flight,
Toil is mere game!

2
The sun casts laurel-shade,
The friendly breeze complies,
Offering twenty years of fame
For one happy day!

3
From Virgil's crafted lays
Man's inspiration rises still...
He gave twenty years of toil
For one creative day!

Nerves

Yesterday I went to a place
Where people die of hunger;
Inspecting tomb-like rooms
I slipped on an unpredicted stair.

It must have been a miracle, surely it was,
That I clutched at a rotten plank
(In it a nail as in the arms of a *cross!*...)
I escaped with my life!

But carried away only half my heart.
Of mirth ? Barely a trace!
I bypassed the crowd like a cattle mart,
I was sick of the world...

Today I must call on the Baroness
Who, sitting on a satin couch,
Entertains with largesse –
But tell her what?

                    Mirrors will crack,
Candelabra shudder at the *realism*
And painted parrots
From beak to beak cry *'Socialism!'*
Along the length of the ceiling.

So: I will take a seat
Hat in hand, then put it down,
And when the party's done,
Go home a silent hypocrite.

The last despotism

'What news?' – 'Despotism's abolished!...I have it all:
And here's the *despatch*...'
                              'I trust you are well –
Be seated – *despatch*...*it says?*...Do take a chair!
But wait – I hear a mackintosh swishing in the hall –
Someone's coming! – It's the Baron – recovered from his fall...
Please sit! – What news can the Baron share...?'

                    *

'And that *despatch*...it says what...? A sugared drink?
Or perhaps an orange?...' 'In Greece –
Locusts – on Cyprus a village slipped over the brink –
Adelina Patti's singing in *The Golden Fleece* –
I see the orange's from Malta – it's very sweet.'
'Have another...'

                    *

'...and how is Despotism in defeat??'

                    *

But they've just announced the ex-chamberlain's bride
And her adopted son – 'What's your view of *nepotism?*
The boy's older than his mother by a year and a head...
Here they are...
                    ...and now, this Despotism...'

Tell her what ?

1
Tell her – what?...Ah! win her admiration
With not much to say;
Something – of general truths: as that day
And night mean the earth's full rotation!

2
That...during a single pulse-rate
The earth orbits through millions of miles –
The axis poles eternally grate:
Time – stirs the void – –

3
That a year – means whole nature's tremor,
That the seasons – not simply
How waters melt and freeze
And that a heart beats for only an hour.

4
Tell her that...
                    ...then discuss the weather –
Where is it warmer? Colder where?
And add – what the fashion is this year
And not a word more.

[1868]

To Madame M. going to buy a plate

1

There are generations, cities and tribes
    Melancholy and old –
Which have bequeathed not marvels and gold
    But – a handful of pots!

2

In a museum just such a pot
    Attracts a lady with a parasol;
In Sicily she treads (and she is a Pole!)
    Upon she known not what!...

3

While tribes one can't even mourn
    In their anonymous state
Vanish – like a butler after handing
    Her ladyship a plate.

[The 3rd day of 1869, with a plate]

Lapidaria

SCULPTOR:

Sculpture's
Whole secret:
A spirit – like a spark
In gesture caught –
Marvels and wonders
And lifts its tiny palms
From this world's cradle
Towards the still uncaptured
In infinite space!

Only she who nurses
And he who's held a knife;
Only she who dances
And he who's held an arm:
They only – and the earth's
Bosom sensing rain –
Move the spirit's veil
In a joyful refrain!

MAECENAS:

Since, master sculptor,
You so comprehend art's curious *mystery*,
Let Valerie, my late wife,
Have a monument from you knife –
Let there be a stony angel
In a praying pose
Gazing at the base
Towards two crests
Crowned with a rose,
So that each feeling breast
Should sigh from the heart
And say (in a formula):
'God grant her rest!'

[1876]

'Give me a blue ribbon...'

Give me a blue ribbon – I will hand it back
Without delay...
Or give me your shadow with your supple neck;
– No! not the shadow.

The shadow will change when your hand moves,
It tells no lie.
Now there is nothing I want from you,
I take my arm away.

In the past God healed my wounds
With lesser things:
A leaf stuck to a window pane,
A drop of rain.

Aphorisms*

Polish bread has a bitter taste.

No one can destroy a nation without the co-operation of that nation's citizens.

A nation bleeding only because for the past hundred years its every action came too early and every book too late.

Is there any other nation which has undertaken so many untimely sacrifices of its blood, property and intellect ?

A nation consists not just of what distinguishes it from other nations, but also of what binds it to other nations.

Truth in life, not just in knowledge.

You can drink from a carafe if you grip its neck and press it to your lips, but if you wish to drink from a spring, you must go on your knees and bow your head.

Imitation of those who have introduced something concerning the overall development of man is not imitation but humanity.

No virtue is so rare and splendid that it cannot be misused.

Although there is nothing absolutely new, yet everything which is shown at the proper time is absolutely new.

It is better that you should lose your life beneath a shattered tree which you had once planted – than that you should wander in the desert, regarding mirages as your own orchards.

* Norwid was not a conscious aphorist but aphoristic phrases, sentences and paragraphs feature prominently in his various prose writings. In 1947 the eminent critic Wacław Borowy compiled an anthology of Norwid's 'Thoughts' which has served as an inspiration for the above translations. [Ed.]

To have a heart one must use it.

A spirit is like water – you sweep it from the hills into a valley and it will erupt into the sky by the measure of its debasement.

To love – without covering up your eyes – that really is an art.

We must guard not only against evil men but also against those who are unable to understand us.

I have seen carrots and turnips in beautifully cooked broth, the carrots and turnips cut into the most elegant patterns: stars and numbers, burning hearts, crosses even...!
All the same, carrots and turnips remained carrots and turnips.

LEOPOLD STAFF

Leopold Staff was born in Lwów, the chief cultural centre in south-east Poland, now part of the Soviet Union. At the university there he studied law, philosophy and Romance languages and in 1900 published his first poems in a student magazine. After World War I he moved to Warsaw where he spent the rest of his long life.

Between 1901 and 1954 Staff published sixteen books of poetry; a seventeenth volume, planned by the poet, appeared posthumously in 1958. Staff received several state awards, honorary doctorates from Warsaw and Kraków and a PEN Club prize for his achievement as a translator of numerous philosophical and literary classics.

Staff was the benign spirit who presided over Polish poetry during the first half of this century. He remained serenely aloof from all movements and schools and achieved the seemingly impossible: general and critical acclaim and the respect and admiration of fellow-poets.

' "But, dear lady, what use is all that poetry? My late husband thought that one of the boys would carry on the business and develop it, but he was disappointed. Poldzio [Leopold] writes poems but he is sickly and weak and I too am not what I used to be...The worst crowd are the painters. Dear friend, if you could see these artists, their bottoms shining through their trousers, holes in their shoes, hair long, matted and dirty. At first the poet Kasprowicz would offer them hospitality, but in the end his wife found it all too much and threw them out. It was then that our Poldzio took pity on them and brought them to our house. They often stay several days at a time. We have to give them food and drink. I haven't enough beds or linen, so they sleep on the floor. There is so much bother, so much cleaning that I've tried to get rid of them a number of times, but Poldzio gets irritated and won't let me. I've often told him that we shall get lice from these drunken friends of his, but that leaves him cold. He tells me they are very talented individuals temporarily facing hard times. But, my dear lady, don't I face hard times?"

'When she finished, Mrs Staff wiped her tears with a handkerchief, said goodbye and I never saw her again. She died in Lwów in 1919.' (Jan Sobota)

'At the Staff celebration organised in 1967 the great hall of Warsaw University could not hold all his admirers. The audience consisted of those who knew him personally, of academics and scholars and of crowds of young people for whom Staff meant only his poetry. Staff's poetry had accompanied the young who worshipped the now-forgotten Przybyszewski [1868-1927], his poetry was recited with

deep feeling by the admirers of the pre-war Skamander poets, and
the quietly reflective poems of *Still weather* [1946] reminded those
who grew up in the nightmare of Hitlerian terror in those days of
total annihilation of all that was beautiful, all that was human.' (To-
masz Jodełka-Burzecki)

Awakening

It's dawn,
But there is no light.
I am half-awake,
A mess all round.
I ought to tie up this,
Connect that
And reach a decision.
I know nothing.
I can't find my shoes,
I can't find myself.
I have a headache.

A song

They order me to mount the tower
Upon a brazen horn to blow
In praise of fearsome knights
And a bloody armoured show.

But the tower's crumbling,
Spit chokes the horn,
There is chiselling, rumbling
And scraping all round.

In truth, I really can't
Make the horn sing –
If pressed, I just might
Handle a bow and string.

So in my garden, like the birds,
I hum a song by the fence
Where they're digging spuds
And will be planting beans.

Faun

A graceful marble faun
In a skipping pose
Plays upon a flute,
His head lies on the lawn.

With mould overspread
It stares dumbly into space,
Proving that a song
Does not require a head.

Although during midday heat
Poets yearn for leafy bowers,
Looking insulted and cross
They avoid this retreat.

Sky at night

A black night, silver night.
A world boundless
In space and time.
In the centre, a milky way.
Who passes there?
That surpasses human understanding.

Problems

You don't solve problems.
You experience them
Like days which, once passed, are gone.
Like old clothes
You've outgrown
Slipping off your shoulders
And you enter
The final door naked and free
Like the dawn.

In an old house

In an old house below the threshold
Dark stairs lead down
To a den in the cellar
Smelling of fustiness and sour wine.
Amid brick-red walls like raw meat
With verdigris mildew stains
A candle set in a hollowed-out turnip
Casts a wavering light on a trio of ruffians,
Mercenaries or cutpurses.
Two sit illumined at a table
On rough benches facing each other;
Beneath their gleaming armour plate
They wear leather jerkins,
Rapiers and hunting knives at their side,
Heads covered with swashbuckling hats
Sporting a cock's feather.
Both are dishevelled,
One is dark, the other ginger
With bloodshot eyes,
They clutch greasy cards
And now and then reach for a pewter mug
Which they replenish from a copper jug.
The players stare at the cards, exchange furtive glances.
Behind redhead's back and concealed in his shadow
Sits the third of the gang wrapped in a cloak
And gives the dark one surreptitious signs with his hands.
Silence, a moment of tension.
A whiff of a quarrel, a fight, of iron and blood...
...While high above the threshold
In a bleak room, in the cold light of day,
Quiet Baruch Spinoza
Bloodless like his God
Sits pensive at the window
Grinding lenses.

'Once in a while...'
(for Mieczysław Jastrun)

Once in a while
Over many years,
Over decades or centuries
Which lurk in corners
Like silent listeners,
A casual passer-by
Sits down at a table over a book
Cleared of dust and cobwebs,
Whispers quietly,
Smiles and cries.

He shuts the finished book
Placing it on a shelf
Among dusty cobwebs
And departs for ever,
Man the eternal traveller.

Through a barred window
Time and forgetfulness
Enter the library.

Duckweed
(for Jan Parandowski)

In an ancient overgrown park
I stood near a pond
Thick with a coat of weeds.
Thinking
That the water must once have been clear
And that it should be so again
I picked a dry branch
And skimmed the green patina
Guiding it to the weir.

A sober wise man
His brow scored with thought
Surprised me at this task
Saying with a gentle smile
Of condescending rebuke:
'Don't you begrudge the time?
Each moment is a drop of eternity,
Life a twinkling of its eye.
There are so many deserving causes.'

I walked away shamed
And throughout the day
Meditated on life and death,
On Socrates
And the immortal soul,
On the pyramids and Egyptian corn,
I considered the Roman Forum and the moon,
The dinosaur and the Eiffel Tower...
But it all came to nothing.

When I returned the following day
To the same spot
By the green-coated pond
I saw
The wise man, his brow smooth,
Quietly
Skimming the weedy surface
With the branch I had thrown away,
Guiding the green to the weir.

Birds sang in the branches
Trees rustled softly.

LEON ZDZISŁAW STROIŃSKI

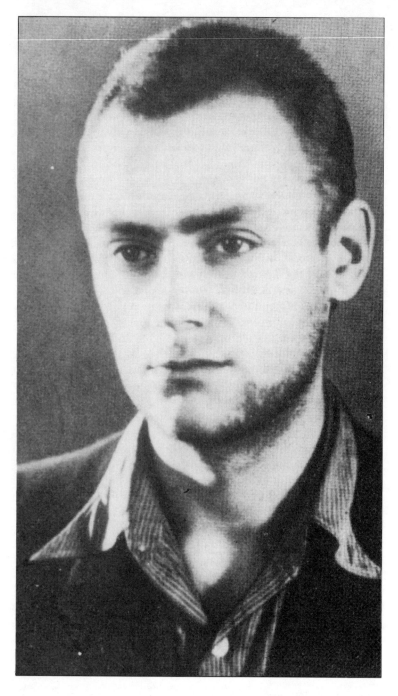

ski53

Leon Zdzisław Stroiński was born in 1921 in Warsaw. He studied law and Polish literature under German occupation at the clandestine Warsaw University. In May 1943, in the company of two other young writers, Wacław Bojarski and Tadeusz Gajcy, he laid a wreath at the Warsaw statue of Copernicus inscribed 'To the Polish genius Nicholas Copernicus on the 400th anniversary of his death – from the Polish Resistance'. During this demonstration Bojarski was killed by a policeman, Gajcy escaped and Stroiński was arrested. He was released two months later thanks to strenuous efforts by his father. He spent the following summer in his parents' house forging German documents for the Resistance. During the Warsaw Rising of 1944 he died in action on 16 August when the Germans blew up the house defended by the contingent he commanded. Gajcy was killed in the same engagement.

Stroiński was not a prolific writer. Some of his work perished in the destruction of Warsaw (including a sequence of prose-poems called *Clouds* or *Mists*), and what has survived, chiefly in wartime publications, was collected in 1963 in a slim volume entitled *Okno* (*Window*) which includes 9 poems, 11 prose poems, a short story and two polemical pieces. A new edition appeared in 1982.

The prose poems deal obsessively with life under the occupation. Stroiński succeeds in capturing that eerie, bizarre and dream-like atmosphere, which perhaps only those who have experienced it can fully appreciate, by the use of startling ramified metaphors and a juxtaposition of stark realism with grim, grotesque expressionism. Stroiński realised, as so few Polish poets were able to do, that this unorthodox, at times lyrical and almost humorous, portrayal of wartime madness is more moving and terrifying than grandiose verbal gestures importuning sympathy and pity.

Stroiński's prose lyrics are a remarkable technical achievement: they are perhaps the best examples in Polish of the full exploitation of this difficult medium since Rimbaud first realised its true potential.

'When during a discussion attention was drawn to the fact that his prose lyrics might be somewhat reminiscent of Jules Supervielle or Max Jacob, Stroiński protested, trying to show the difference of his position and his perception of reality, and in particular a total difference in the material used. This last argument was comparatively the most persuasive: such metaphors could arise only from experience of wartime occupation horror, supplemented at most with readings of a poetry related in form which suited Stroiński's type of imagination.' (Tadeusz Sołtan)

'These prose lyrics, subtle in outline, bold in metaphor, were an attempt to portray the ominous reality. And times were terrible. On 16 October 1943 public executions were started in Warsaw and the city talked of nothing else. Almost daily the Germans pulled people out of trams and transported them to Pawiak gaol to face police tribunals. Posters the colour of dried blood announced lists of hostages and two or three days later almost identical lists of those executed.' (Lesław Bartelski)

Other days

When war broke out – it was a bit like a National Day, but grander than the Third of May or the Eleventh of November – the days were broad and flat, reaching out to the limits of the furthest departures tangled into the whistling of steam-engines.

And earlier still the days, quite rounded, rang rolling on, measured by the school bell.

Those are the days I seek in vain.

And when the taste of those days congealed into bitterness on the lips, I realised they would not return.

Still, moments of the time when I was a pupil in a greenish-golden countryside, or maybe merely dust in the market-place, fly in and alight upon days as narrow as the arrow-slits of ancient walls. Just starlings gone grey in war winters, deprived of nests and sunshine.

But that world has vanished.

In any event it was so tiny it could even have fallen down a crack in the floor-boards.

Or perhaps it had merely flattened itself to a few smudged letters that have outlasted my family and friends.

About war

Over roads of pine logs lorries carry war through the forest. Distant, they raise weapons to their eyes.

On the outskirts, on stalls under yellowish awnings, they sell apples and rainbows.

Motors hum on land, in air and on sea. This even has a certain charm – from Nowy Świat* one can see a deep furrow of green water with which a battleship writes out longings in the English Channel.

In a first-floor window you can also see a girl with closely cropped hair playing with a lame kitten.

Tanks climb a wall of feebly blooming bushes and rattle as though they were carrying skulls and bones.

Houses and towers fall down like hail. A grey-maned horse draws a plough up a slope, the sun and crows alight on turned up stones,

* Main thoroughfare in Warsaw. [Ed.]

and smoke from crematoria sways against a blue sky.

At the same time, at the point where the meadow meets the forest, wartime cadets manoeuvre for an attack.

Now one can see a paper-tissue, an almost-white wing of an angel, who was probably freckled, drooping from telegraph wires.

Lower down a sly-faced cripple plays 'Warszawianka' on a comb.

This is the glassy surface of a still river, but in a moment one of the huge fish tossing in the depths will break the surface.

Warsaw

During the building of the barricades, the Vistula, brimming with reflections of forests, birds and white roads lined with poplars, rose, at first like a mist, then like a stiff cover of a book.

In its shade at dawn caretakers come out with huge frayed brooms to sweep up the tears which have collected during the night and lie thickly in the streets.

Already, the market women, extended to the edge of the sunlight, recommend potatoes grown on graves.

And on the horizon of the street, across the roar of grenades lying in the curves of cobblestones, the soul of the city has been moving for months.

The reflection of her face, too difficult to comprehend, has left a trace on the twisted faces of ruins as on the handkerchief of St Veronica.

Those who will come in the far, far future wanting to decipher them, drawing their cold-blue hands across features taut like strings, and who with careless fingers will poke the moan of those dried up in crevices –

will burst into prayer or blasphemy.

Here my country has come together from decimated forests and villages turned into a dog's howl. It persists in the whisper of mechanised armour.

We had to wait through so much blood and pathos in order to build from the silence of ruined monuments such a vault over a city of jazz and death.

Now lemurs from Gothic temples are thick on roofs of trams and terrify insurance officials on their way home.

The dead wander beneath the pavements and pound on bucklers which give a hollow sound, while at evening in double rows of whispers they walk arm in arm with the living, and you can tell them apart only by the skilfully folded wings, which nevertheless stick out on their backs like humps.

But in daytime huge stone capstans hum, and only around noon, when folk sit down to lunch and it's a bit quieter, can you hear more distinctly the heavy rhythmical tread of God's steel-shod boots.

1944

In a street yellow with horse-manure, round sparrows brimming with surprise hop amid strange shapes, which have dropped from the lips of the dying sealed with plaster of Paris.

A group of people entangled in some old rain like barbed wire hangs about at the street-corner.

A bloated flower-girl in a check shawl squeals 'What a bleeding mob', and elbows her way through the crowd.

As if in reply, a dislodged brick protruding out of dark plaster, creaks lengthily like a well-hoist.

And when the pock-marked wall opposite furrows like a deep river, it's so quiet you can hear how in distant cottages buried in snowdrifts an orange flame plays gingerly on slanting blackened chimneys, and glowing coals fall away hissing.

And above only a streamer of clouds.

And below only the silence of parted lips.

Storm-black Copernicus petrifies above arcades shot through with a drop of blood.

Men and trees grow ponderously amid melting snow, their brows branded with crosses as small as bullets.

Behind them on the horizon a flaming pillar.

The bloated flower-girl in a check shawl again squeals, 'What a bleeding mob'.

Sparrows fly up lightly over a strange homeland which can reveal itself only through gilded rye and birch trees or blood clots amid horse-manure.

But here there is only snow, so white grass blooms and a mother hums a monotonous lullaby to a dead child about a country of prayers and fulfilled curses.

But there – Mickiewicz's iron spasm breaks the shape above the flame and the darkness standing numb

– and a terrible prophecy is fulfilled slowly like a boulder leaning out of its frame.

People on the corner sag heavily like a bridge.

'What a bleeding mob,' squeals the bloated flower-girl in a check shawl.

Father's return

Disturbing the forebodings grating in the corner, I was moving stealthily to open the urn on a chest of drawers. Why did they choose to place the urn with father against a rug which in daytime represents a Hawaian girl under a palm-tree and now – surely something quite unknown?

I had to be wary in case he should ask, 'Why are you wandering about in the night – go to bed.' And yet he must be grey inside that can, so he won't say anything.

And his eyes, bulging and helpless after his glasses had been knocked off, must surely be on the bottom.

Yes. In his letters the words gradually became more and more indistinct, as though they wanted to run off the yellowish page – like ants.

Yes. Father probably turned into dust gradually, so that the words were falling apart when he wrote, 'I am quite well, may God bless…'

But at that time it was quite different. And cigarette smoke would briskly write time on the window panes. The roaring motorcar darkened the world and threw moths, tiny as sparks, into the stiff flame of the lamp. The moment was stretched like an elastic. And I, waiting for it to snap, huddled against the wall. When they started beating him on the face, I noticed that one of them had a gold tooth and I huddled even closer to the wall. Long, long I waited for everything to cool down to a glass ball, no bigger than a fist, which I would then place on the whatnot to gaze on in the evening.

Now I fear that that moment lies blackened somewhere and I might tread on it because the darkness is almost complete.

When I plunged my hand into the ash – it was almost soft and tasted a bit like soap. Just then I heard a company singing in foreign words and the cook started coughing.

TADEUSZ RÓŻEWICZ

Lucky the nation which boasts a poet
And in its travails isn't lost for speech
CZESŁAW MIŁOSZ, 'To Tadeusz Różewicz, Poet'

Tadeusz Różewicz

Tadeusz Różewicz was born in 1921 in Radomsko in central Poland. He joined the Resistance during the War; studied art history in Kraków; and now lives in Wrocław, closely associated with the local theatre. In the English-speaking countries he is chiefly known as perhaps the most outstanding and influential poet of his genera-tion, but he is also a prolific experimental dramatist – he is widely performed in Poland and Continental Europe – and four collections of his plays have been published in England and America.

I have translated well over a hundred of Różewicz's poems and this is a personal selection from that set. I have chosen these shorter poems which, it seemed to me, have most successfully crossed the language barrier. The joys and miseries of translation include the knowledge that it is difficult to asses in advance which text will translate well.

In March 1981 Różewicz read his poetry at Keats House in Hampstead. He greatly enjoyed the occasion because he found a rapport with a responsive audience gathered in the elegant, intimate drawing-room. His pleasure was enhanced when he stepped outside and saw the imposing trees of Keats Grove sharply silhouetted in artificial light.

Trees feature prominently in Różewicz's work. One particular tree in 'Chestnut' represents the world of idealised childhood. 'The world like a tree,' he declares explicitly in another poem where the tree is an Arcadian growth, whose role is destroyed once a war-victim is hung from it. Polish makes no distinction between "tree" and "wood", so in effect Różewicz says 'how thirsty and starved this *tree* is' when describing Christ's cross, thus identifying the suffering tree with the agony of Christ. Trees stand for innocence, life, growth, which is why tree-felling is seen as a horrifying, heart-rending out-rage, while in 'Massacre of the boys' the smoke of Nazi crematoria is described as being

> like a figure of geometry
> a tree of black smoke
> a vertical
> dead tree
> with no star in its crown

This smoke is an obscene parody, a negation of a flourishing, living tree. Nothing could be worse than the rigid stasis of geometrical order. Różewicz presents his affirmation of the world in terms of organic growth, sensual delight and the pleasures of the flesh. If he has come to be known as a bitter war-poet, it is because he has had more experience of tree-felling than of tree-planting.

Doors

A glass of red wine
stands on a table
in a dark room

through the open door
I see a landscape of childhood
a kitchen and a blue kettle
the Sacred Heart
mother's transparent shadow

the crowing cock
in a rounded silence

the first sin
a little white seed
in a green fruit soft
bitterish

the first devil is pink
and moves its hemispheres
under a spotted silk
dress

in the illumined landscape
a third door
opens
and beyond it in a mist
towards the back
a little to the left
or in the centre

I see
nothing

[1966]

The first is hidden

the first tree

I don't remember
its name
nor the landscape
where it grew

I don't remember
whether I came to know it
with my eye
or ear
whether it was a rustle
a scent or a hue

whether it appeared
in sunlight
or in snow

the first animal

I don't remember
its voice warmth
shape

all animals
have their names

only that first one
is hidden
unknown

[1965]

Chestnut

Saddest of all is leaving
home on an autumn morning
when there is no hope of an early return

The chestnut father planted in front
of the house grows in our eyes

mother is tiny
you could carry her in your arms

On the shelf
jars full of preserves
like sweet-lipped goddesses
have retained the flavour
of eternal youth

soldiers at the back of the drawer
will stay leaden till the end of the world

while God almighty who mixed in
bitterness into the sweetness
hangs on the wall helpless
and badly painted

childhood is like the worn face
on a golden coin that rings
true.

Photograph

today I received an old card
from a distant country
a picture of Erbalunga

I had never heard that name
I don't know where it is
and I don't wish to know

Erbalunga

yesterday I received
mother's photograph
saved from 1944

in the photograph
mother is still young beautiful
smiling faintly

but on the reverse
I read words written
in her own hand
'1944 terrible for me'

in 1944
the Gestapo
had murdered my elder brother

we hid his death
from mother
but she saw through us
and hid it
from us

[1979]

'But whoever sees...'

But whoever sees my mother
in a purple smock in a white hospital
trembling
stiffening
with a wooden smile
and white gums

who for fifty years had faith
but now weeps and says
'I don't know...I don't know'

her face is like a large smudged tear
she clasps her hands like a frightened
little girl
her lips are blue

but whoever sees my mother
a hounded little animal
with a bulging eye

he

oh I would like to bear her upon my heart
and nourish her with sweetness

[1947-48]

The return

Suddenly the window will open
and mother will call
it's time to come in

the wall will part
I will enter heaven in muddy shoes

I will come to the table
and answer questions rudely

I am all right leave me
alone. Head in hand I
sit and sit. How can I tell them
about that long
and tangled way.

Here in heaven mothers
knit green scarves

flies buzz

father dozes by the stove
after six days' labour.

No – surely I can't tell them
that men are at each
other's throats.

Wood

A wooden Christ
from a mediaeval Mystery play
goes on all fours

full of red splinters

he has a collar of thorns
and the bowed head
of a beaten dog

how thirsty and starved this wood is

Pigtail

When all the women in the transport
had their heads shaved
four workmen with brooms made of birch twigs
swept up
and gathered up the hair

Behind clean glass
the stiff hair lies
of those suffocated in gas chambers
there are pins and side combs
in this hair

The hair is not shot through with light
is not parted by the breeze
is not touched by any hand
or rain or lips

In huge chests
clouds of dry hair
of those suffocated
and a faded plait
a pigtail with a ribbon
pulled at school
by naughty boys.

[The Museum, Auschwitz, 1948]

Massacre of the boys

The children cried 'Mummy!
But I have been good!
It's dark in here! Dark!'

See them They are going to the bottom
See the small feet
they went to the bottom Do you see
that print
of a small foot here and there

pockets bulging
with string and stones
and little horses made of wire

A great plain closed
like a figure of geometry
and a tree of black smoke
a vertical
dead tree
with no star in its crown.

[The Museum, Auschwitz, 1948]

A tree

Happy were
the poets of old
the world like a tree
they like a child

What shall I hang
upon the branch of a tree
which has suffered
a rain of steel

Happy were
the poets of old
around the tree
they danced like a child

What shall I hang
upon the branch of a tree
which is burnt
and never will sing

Happy were
the poets of old
beneath the oak
they sang like a child

But our tree
creaked in the night
with the weight
of a corpse despised

Love 1944

Naked defenceless
lips upon lips
eyes
wide open

listening

we drifted
across a sea
of tears and blood

[1954]

The survivor

I am twenty-four
led to slaughter
I survived.

The following are empty synonyms:
man and beast
love and hate
friend and foe
darkness and light.

The ways of killing men and beasts are the same
I've seen them:
truckfuls of chopped-up men
who will not be saved.

Ideas are mere words:
virtue and crime
truth and lies
beauty and ugliness
courage and cowardice.

Virtue and crime weigh the same
I've seen it:
in a man who was both
criminal and virtuous.

I seek a teacher and a master
may he restore my sight hearing and speech
may he once more name ideas and objects
may he separate darkness from light.

I am twenty-four
led to slaughter
I survived.

In the midst of life

After the end of the world
after death
I found myself in the midst of life
creating myself
building life
people animals landscapes

this is a table I said
this is a table
there is bread and a knife on the table
knife serves to cut bread
people are nourished by bread

man must be loved
I learnt by night and day
what must one love
I would reply man

this is a window I said
this is a window
there is a garden beyond the window
I see an apple tree in the garden
the apple tree blossoms
the blossom falls
fruit is formed
ripens

my father picks the apple
the man who picks the apple
is my father

I sat on the threshold

that old woman who
leads a goat on a string
is needed more
is worth more

than the seven wonders of the world
anyone who thinks or feels
she is not needed
is a mass murderer

this is a man
this is a tree this is bread

people eat to live
I kept saying to myself
human life is important
human life has great importance
the value of life
is greater than the value of all things
which man has created
man is a great treasure
I repeated stubbornly

this is water I said
I stroked the waves with my hand
and talked to the river
water I would say
nice water
this is me

man talked to water
talked to the moon
to the flowers and to rain
talked to the earth
to the birds
to the sky

the sky was silent
the earth was silent
and if a voice was heard
flowing
from earth water and sky
it was a voice of another man

[1955]

They shed the load

He comes to you
and says

you are not responsible
either for the world or the end of the world
the load has been lifted off your shoulders
you are like children and birds
go, play

and they play

they forget
that contemporary poetry
means struggle for breath

[1959]

Draft for a contemporary love poem

For surely whiteness
is best described through greyness
bird through stone
sunflowers
in December

in the past love poems
described flesh
described this and that
eyelashes for instance

surely redness
should be described
through greyness sun through rain
poppies in November
lips at night

the most telling
description of bread
is one of hunger
it includes
the damp porous centre
the warm interior
sunflowers at night
breast belly thighs of Cybele

a spring-like
transparent description
of water
is the description of thirst
of ashes
desert
it conjures up a mirage
clouds and trees enter
the mirror

Hunger deprivation
absence
of flesh
is the description of love
the contemporary love poem

[Summer 1963]

New comparisons

To what will you compare
day
is it like night
to what will you compare
an apple
is it like a kingdom
to what will you compare
flesh
at night
the silence
between lips
between
to what will you compare an eye
a hand in darkness
is the right like the left
teeth tongue mouth
a kiss
to what will you compare
a hip
hair
fingers
breath
silence
poetry
in daylight
at night

Autumnal

When it rains
I lie flat extended expansively far
in a mist

I feel stretched beneath the skin
moist twigs of blackthorn
prickly and dark

the hairy blood-vessels
of plant stems

blood flows upwards rust
bile verdigris
and colours the plain

on the rim
of the coal basin
a horse and plough
form a pastoral composition
extensive forgotten

Laughter

The cage stayed shut
until a bird was hatched inside

the bird remained mute
until the cage
rusting in the silence
opened

silence lasted until
behind black wires
we heard laughter

Death

Wall window
outside
a child's tiny voice

below the window a street
a tram
King Herod enters
devil death

I give the King sixpence
and chase away
the whole crowd

death
is real
looks back
shakes her finger

Penetration

death
penetrated life
like light
through a cobweb
hanging in an open doorway

now on his death-bed
he was moving out
shouting plotting stratagems
temporising

death was eating up the features
of successive faces layered
on the bone

Proofs

Death will not correct
a single line of verse
she is no proof-reader
she is no sympathetic
lady editor

a bad metaphor is immortal

a shoddy poet who has died
is a shoddy dead poet

a bore bores after death
a fool keeps up his foolish chatter
from beyond the grave

Picture

Who will recognise him

mother father brothers
that other woman perhaps
whose face
in a clouded mirror
flows down like rain

and you
when you look at yourself
what do you see

I see a man created
in the image and likeness of a god
who's gone

[1979]

'That rustle...'

That rustle

life pouring
from a world full of objects
into death

it's through me
like a hole
in reality
this world pushes through
into the next

I think this through to the end
he whom
I sought above
waits below

in a burrow
a transfiguration

languid braying
of trumpets kneaded
out of waste-paper
rolled out of
newsprint

a rising from the dead
absentminded
futile

[1976]

Grass

I grow
in the bondings of walls
where they are
joined
there where they meet
there where they are vaulted

there I penetrate
a blind seed
scattered by the wind

patiently I spread
in the cracks of silence
I wait for the walls to fall
and return to earth

then I will cover
names and faces

[1962]

Tree-felling
(in memory of Jarosław Iwaszkiewicz, author of 'Gardens')

A ceaseless anxiety
reigns among the crowns

a tree scored
for felling
with a white mark of annihilation
was still breathing
its boughs and branches
clawing
at the fleeting clouds

the leaves trembled and withered
sensing death

Trees don't move
from place to place
in search of nourishment
they can't escape
the saw
and the axe

a ceaseless anxiety
reigns among the crowns

tree-cutting is an execution
void of ceremony

spitting sawdust
the mechanical saw
enters the bark the pulp and the core
like lightning

struck at its side
it collapsed
and fell into the undergrowth
with its dead weight
it squashed grass and herbs
slender light blades
and trembling gossamer

together with the tree
they destroyed its shade
transparent
ambiguous
image
sign
appearing
in the light
of the sun and moon

The diligent roots
have yet no inkling
of the loss of the trunk
and crown

slowly
the surface death of the tree
reaches below ground

the roots of neighbouring trees
touch
enter into relationships
and bonds

beside men and beast
the only living sentient beings
created in the image
and likeness of gods

Trees
cannot hide from us

Children born
painlessly in clinics
maturing
in discotheques
torn apart by artificial light
and sound
gaping at TV screens
do not converse
with trees

Trees of childhood cut burnt
poisoned dead
turn green over our heads
in May
shed leaves on graves
in November
grow within us
unto death

[February 1981]

Description of a poem

I tried to remember
that ideal
unwritten
poem

nearly ripe
shaped in the night
tangible
it was sinking
and dissolving in the light of day
it did not
exist

at times I felt it
on the tip of the tongue
anxiously
I would sit down pen
in hand
waiting patiently
until convinced
it was an illusion
I would walk away

the poem was probably
a poem about itself
as a pearl
speaks of pearls
and a butterfly of butterflies

it was neither a love-poem
nor an elegy

it neither mourned
nor praised
it neither described
nor judged

that poem
which eludes me in daylight
has hidden itself in itself
only sometimes
I feel its bitterness
and internal warmth
but I don't pull it out of
the dark hollow depth
on to the flat bank
of reality

unborn
it fills the emptiness
of a disintegrating world
with unknown speech

[1981]

TYMOTEUSZ KARPOWICZ

Tymoteusz Karpowicz was born in 1921 near Wilno, now capital of the Lithuanian Socialist Republic within the Soviet Union, university town of Mickiewicz, Słowacki and Miłosz, to name but a few.

'Little known before the political upheavals of 1956 in Poland, Karpowicz made his initial mark in 1957 with *Gorzkie źródła (Bitter springs)*, a slim collection of poems of breathtaking freshness and beauty. There was a new vision in them, both strange and familiar, intensely personal and universal, and quite unlike anything seen in Poland since the death of Leśmian. Each subsequent volume only confirmed Karpowicz's original talent...He is a difficult poet to read and even in the original often reads like a major foreign, preferably English, poet badly translated. Probably so, because he seems to push Polish to its very limits and, sometimes, to what would appear to be beyond its limits.' (Jan Darowski)

'['Lesson in silence'] is an example of how it is possible to achieve naked expression through purity of diction, and how avant-garde poetics can be modified through the use of near-parabolic structure to support statements that are, ultimately, political in nature...
'Perhaps more than any other poet in Poland in the post-war period, Karpowicz derives his poetic impulses from the modernist tradition, from the Mallarméan pursuit of the absolute poem and, more immediately, from Julian Przyboś [1901-1970] and Bolesław Leśmian [1877-1937], both of whom, although in very different

ways, aimed at making the utmost possible distinction between poetic language and prose.' (Bogdan Czaykowski)

I hope that in my translations Karpowicz does not sound like a 'major foreign, preferably Polish, poet badly translated'. I have prudently confined myself to his earlier work in which there is hardly a hint, except perhaps in 'Ecclesiastes', of the subsequent explorations of language which reached a formidable density in the ambitious 400-page sequence *Odwrócone światło (Reversed light)* (1972).

Karpowicz left Poland in 1973 and since 1978 has been in charge of Polish Language and Literature at the University of Illinois at Chicago Circle. He has not published any poetry since 1972.

Lesson in silence

Whenever a butterfly
folded its wings
too violently –
they cried: quiet please!

If but the wing
of a scared bird
brushed a sunray –
they cried: silence please!

Thus they taught
elephants to walk
noiselessly over a drum
man over earth

Trees rose
soundlessly in the field
as hair does
in terror

False alarm

The cry
brought out neighbours
then the ambulance
and the police

But the street's stone flowed clear
no hands were bloodstained
no heart lead-packed

They dispersed
declared the alarm false –

As if only blood and lead
revealed to men
man's agony

Dream

What terrible dream
caused the poet
to jump out of his sleep
like a stag from a burning forest?

– The butterfly in his metaphor
had veiled him with its wings

and the door-knob he had described
twitched

Ecclesiastes

there is a time of opening the eyes and closing the bed
time of donning a shirt and shedding sleep
time of drowsy soap and half-awakened skin
time of the hair-brush and of sparks in the hair
time of trouser-legs time of shoe-laces time of buttons
of laddered stockings of the slipper's blindness
time of the fork and of the knife time of sausages and boiled eggs
time of the tram time of the conductress time of the policeman
time of good morning and time of goodbye
time of carrots peas and parsley
of tomato soup and shepherd's pie
time of trussing chicken and releasing forbidden speeds of thought
time of a cinema ticket or a ticket to nowhere
to a river perhaps perhaps to a cloud
there is finally a time of closed eyelids and the open bed
time of past present and future
praesens historicum and plusquamperfectum
time perfect and imperfect
time from wall to wall

WISŁAWA SZYMBORSKA

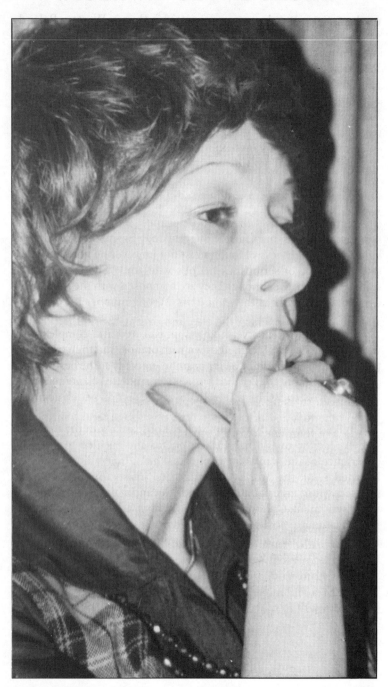

Wisława Szymborska was born in 1923 in Bnin in Western Poland. She abandoned the sociology course at Kraków University when its independence was destroyed by Stalinism. She has published several collections of poetry and her *Selected Poems* appeared in 1973.

If there is a feminist tradition in Polish poetry which Szymborska is following, it is that of Maria Pawlikowska-Jasnorzewska (who died in Manchester in 1945) and whose characteristic 'La précieuse' reads:

> I see you tucked in your furs,
> poised over a tiny puddle,
> a pekinese under your arm, an umbrella and a rose...
> And how will you step into infinity?

It is a tradition of wit, charm and elegance, feminine, rather than feminist. But this may falsely suggest that Szymborska's work is lightweight. Lightness of touch must not however be here mistaken for an absence of seriousness. 'Lot's wife' and 'The terrorist' are sombre enough, even though they are composed with the same cool, detached assurance as the *jeu d'ésprit* 'Wrong number'.

'Szymborska is a sensitive, highly sophisticated and complex poet who "borrows words weighed down with pathos, and then tries hard to make them appear light". Her position, not only as the best woman poet in contemporary Poland, but also as a poetic phenomenon on a par with Różewicz, Herbert or Białoszewski, is now widely acknowledged...

'Unlike Różewicz, Szymborska is not obsessed with the theme of war. Already in one of her earliest poems she decided to treat her experience of the war as an intellectual gain: 'our war booty is the knowledge of the world.'...Thus, she insists on being wisely amused, wittily entertaining and readable, and at times allows herself to be sentimental, although seldom without a touch of irony. She likes to assume a *persona* of a keen and ironic observer of the phenomenon of man, and to couch her observations in almost anthropological terms.' (Bogdan Czaykowski)

Portrait of a woman

Must present alternatives.
Change, but on condition that nothing changes.
That is easy, impossible, difficult, worth trying.
Her eyes are, as required, now deep blue, now grey,
black, sparkling, unaccountably filled with tears.
She sleeps with him as one of many, as the one and only.
She'll bear him four children, no children, one.
Naïve, but gives best advice.
Weak, but she'll carry.
She has no head, so she'll have a head,
reads Jaspers and women's magazines.
Has no clue what that nut is for and will build a bridge.
Young, young as usual, always still young.
Holds in her hands a sparrow with a broken wing,
her own money for a long and distant journey,
a chopper, a poultice and a glass of vodka.
Where is she running, perhaps she's tired.
But no, only a little, very, it's no matter.
She either loves him or she's just stubborn.
For better, for worse and for love of God.

Lot's wife

I looked back supposedly curious.
But besides curiosity I might have had other reasons.
I looked back regretting the silver dish.
Through carelessness – tying a sandal strap.
In order not to keep staring at the righteous nape
of my husband, Lot.
Because of sudden conviction that had I died.
He wouldn't have stopped.
Being humble yet disobedient.
Listening for pursuers.
Touched with silence, hoping God had changed His mind.
Our two daughters were already disappearing beyond the hilltop.
I felt my age. Distance,
futility of wandering. Drowsiness.

I looked back when setting down the bundle.
I looked back in terror where to step next.
My path suddenly teeming with snakes,
spiders, field mice and baby vultures.
Now neither good nor evil – just everything living
crawled and hopped in crowded panic.
I looked back in desolation.
Ashamed of running away in stealth.
Wanting to scream, to turn back.
Or only when a gust of wind
untied my hair and lifted up my skirts.
I had a feeling they were watching from the walls of Sodom
with bursts of hearty laughter again and again.
I looked back in anger.
To savour their perdition.
I looked back willessly.
It was only a rock slipping, growling beneath me.
It was a crevice suddenly cut my way off.
A hamster trotted on the edge, raised on two paws
And then it was we both looked back.
No, no. I ran on,
I crawled and I soared
until darkness crashed from heaven
and with it hot gravel and dead birds.
Losing breath I often swerved.
If anyone saw me, would have thought I was dancing.
Conceivably, my eyes were open.

In praise of my sister

My sister doesn't write poems,
and I don't think she'll suddenly start writing poems.
She is like her mother who didn't write poems,
and like her father, who didn't write poems either.
Under my sister's roof I feel safe:
my sister's husband would rather die than write poems.
And – this begins to sound like a found poem –
none of my relations is engaged in writing poems.

There are no old poems in my sister's files
and there aren't any new ones in her handbag.
And when my sister invites me to lunch,
I know she has no plans to read me her poems.
Her soups are excellently improvised,
there is no coffee spilt on her manuscripts.

There are many families where no one writes poems,
but where they do – it's rarely just one person.
Sometimes poetry splashes down in cascades of generations,
creating terrible whirlpools in mutual feelings.

My sister cultivates a quite good spoken prose
and her writing's restricted to holiday postcards,
the text promising the same each year:
that when she returns
she'll tell us
all
all
all about it.

Homecoming

He was back. Said nothing.
But it was clear something had upset him.
He lay down in his suit.
Hid his head under the blanket.
Drew up his knees.
He's about forty, but not at this moment.
He exists – but only as much as in his mother's belly
behind seven skins, in protective darkness.
Tomorrow he is lecturing on homeostasis
in metagalactic space travel.
But now he's curled up and fallen asleep.

A contribution on pornography

There is no debauchery worse than thought.
This wantonness is rampant like a wind-blown weed
on a bed reserved for begonias.

For those who think, nothing is sacred.
Brazenly calling everything by name,
perverse analyses, meretricious syntheses,
wild and dissolute pursuit of naked facts,
lustful petting of sensitive subjects,
a spawning ground of opinions – that's just what they're after.

On a clear day, under cover of darkness,
they consort in pairs, triangles and rings.
No constraint on age or sex of partners.
Friends corrupt friends.
Degenerate daughters deprave their fathers.
Their eyes gleam, their cheeks glow.
A brother pimps for his younger sister.

They prefer the fruit
of the forbidden tree of knowledge
to pink boobs in illustrated mags –
that essentially simple-minded pornography.
The books that divert them have no pictures,
their sole pleasure are special sentences
scored with thumbnail or crayon.

In what shocking positions
with what licentious simplicity
mind can impregnate mind!
Positions unknown even to the Kama Sutra.
During these trysts only tea is steaming.
People sit on chairs, move their lips.
Each crosses his own legs.
So one foot touches the floor,
the other swings free.
But occasionally someone gets up
goes to the window
and through a chink in the curtains
watches the street.

In praise of dreams

In my dream
I paint like Vermeer of Delft.

I speak fluent Greek
and not just with the living.

I drive a car
which obeys me.

I am gifted,
I compose epic verse.

I hear voices
as clearly as genuine saints.

My piano performances
would simply amaze you.

I fly the way prescribed,
that is, out of myself.

Falling off a roof
I know how to land softly on the lawn.

Breathing under water
is no problem.

I'm not complaining:
I managed to discover Atlantis.

It's a pleasure always
to wake before death.

Immediately war starts
I turn over to a better side.

I exist, but don't have to be
a child of the times.

Some years ago
I saw two suns.

And the day before yesterday a penguin.
As clearly as this.

Wrong number

A telephone's been ringing in a gallery room
at midnight when there's no one there;
had there been someone sleeping, he'd now be aware,
but here are only sleepless bards of doom,
only kings grown pale in the light of the moon,
holding their breath and with a vacant look,
while the seemingly lively wife of a crook
stares fixedly at that ringing box,
but no, no, she doesn't move her arm,
she's caught, mutely passive, like the rest
haughtily absent, robed or undressed,
who inattentively ignore the alarm,
displaying, I swear it, greater black humour
than if the chamberlain himself had left the frame
(though nothing save silence rings in his ears).
And as regards the fact that someone in town
is naïvely not putting the receiver down,
having dialled wrongly – he lives and therefore errs.

Perfect

– *Thou art perfect, then, our ship hath touch'd upon*
The deserts of Bohemia? Aye, my lord.
That's from Shakespeare, who, I'm perfect,
was not someone else. Some facts, a date,
a portrait near contemporary...Not enough? Should one await
the proof already snatched up by the Great Sea and hurled
upon Bohemian beaches of this world ?

Theatrical impressions

In tragedy I find the sixth act most important:
when they arise from stage battlefields,
adjust their wigs and robes,
pull out the knife from the breast,
remove the noose from the neck,
stand in line amongst the living
facing the audience.

Bows individual and collective:
a white hand on a wounded heart,
a suicide curtseying,
a beheaded nodding.

Bows in pairs:
fury offering an arm to gentleness,
the victim gazing blissfully in the torturer's eyes,
the revolutionary ungrudgingly marching with the tyrant.

Eternity pressed by the toe of a golden slipper.
Morals dispersed with the brim of a hat.
An incorrigible readiness to repeat it all tomorrow.

A file of those who died much earlier
in acts three and four and between the acts.
The miraculous return of those vanished without trace.

The thought that in the wings they patiently waited
not shedding their costumes
not taking off their make-up
moves me more than tragic tirades.

But truly uplifting is the falling curtain
and what can still be glimpsed beneath it:
here a hand hastily grabs a flower,
there another snatches a dropped sword.
Only then a third, unseen,
accomplishes its task:
grips me by the throat.

The terrorist, he watches

The bomb will explode in the bar at twenty past one.
Now it's only sixteen minutes past.
Some will still have time to enter,
some to leave.

The terrorist's already on the other side.
That distance protects him from all harm
and well it's like the pictures:

A woman in a yellow jacket, she enters.
A man in dark glasses, he leaves.
Boys in jeans, they're talking.
Sixteen minutes past and four seconds.
The smaller one he's lucky, mounts his scooter,
but that taller chap he walks in.

Seventeen minutes and forty seconds.
A girl, she walks by, a green ribbon in her hair.
But that bus suddenly hides her.
Eighteen minutes past.
The girl's disappeared.
Was she stupid enough to go in, or wasn't she.
We shall see when they bring out the bodies.

Nineteen minutes past.
No one else appears to be going in.
On the other hand, a fat bald man leaves.
But seems to search his pockets and
at ten seconds to twenty past one
he returns to look for his wretched gloves.

It's twenty past one.
Time, how it drags.
Surely, it's now.
No, not quite.
Yes, now.
The bomb, it explodes.

Funeral

– so suddenly, who could have guessed
– nerves and cigarettes, I did warn him
– passably, thank you
– unwrap those flowers
– in his brother's case it was the heart, must be in the family
– I would never recognise you with that beard
– only himself to blame, always mixed up in something
– that new one was to speak, can't see him
– Kazek's in Warsaw, Tadek's abroad
– only you were clever enough to take an umbrella
– he was the ablest – doesn't matter now
– it's a connecting room, Basia won't agree
– yes, he was right, but that's no excuse
– door varnishing included – guess how much
– two yolks, a spoonful of sugar
– not his business, shouldn't have meddled
– only in blue and only in small sizes
– five times and never any answer
– all right, I could have, and so could you
– at least she held down that little job
– no idea, probably relatives
– the priest's quite a Belmondo
– I've never been in this part of the cemetery
– I dreamt about him last week, had a premonition
– the daughter is quite pretty
– we're all in the same boat
– condolences to the widow, must rush
– but it used to sound more dignified in Latin
– it's all in the past now
– goodbye, Marta
– let's find a beer somewhere
– give me a ring, we'll talk
– catch a 4 or a 12
– I go this way
– we go over there

Miracle mart

Common miracle:
the happening of many common miracles.

Ordinary miracle:
invisible dogs barking
in the silence of the night.

A miracle among many:
a tiny ethereal cloud
able to cover a large heavy moon.

Several miracles in one:
an alder reflected in water
moreover turned from left to right
moreover growing crown downwards
yet not reaching the bottom
though the waters are shallow.

An everyday miracle:
soft gentle breezes
gusting during storms.

Any old miracle:
cows are cows.

And another like it:
just this particular orchard
from just this pip.

Miracle without frock coat or top hat:
a scattering of white doves.

Miracle – what else would you call it:
today the sun rose at 3.14
and will set at 20.01.

Miracle which doesn't sufficiently amaze:
though the hand has fewer than six fingers
yet it has more than four.

Miracle – just look around:
the world ever-present.

An extra miracle, just as everything is extra:
what is unthinkable
is thinkable.

People on a bridge

A strange planet with its strange people.
They yield to time but don't recognise it.
They have ways of expressing their protest,
they make pictures, like this one for instance:

At first glance, nothing special.
You see water.
You see a shore.
You see a boat sailing laboriously upstream.
You see a bridge over the water and people on the bridge.
The people are visibly quickening their step,
because a downpour has just started
lashing sharply from a dark cloud.

The point is that nothing happens next.
The cloud doesn't change its colour or shape.
The rain neither intensifies nor stops.
The boat sails on motionless.
The people on the bridge
Run just where they were a moment past.
It's difficult to avoid remarking here:
this isn't by any means an innocent picture.
Here time has been stopped.
Its laws have been ignored.
It's been denied influence on developing events.
It's been insulted and spurned.

Thanks to a rebel,
a certain Hiroshige Utagawa
(a creature which as it happens

has long since and quite properly passed away)
time stumbled and fell.

Maybe this was a whim of no significance,
a freak covering just a pair of galaxies,
but we should perhaps add the following:

Here it's considered proper
to regard this little picture highly,
admire it and thrill to it from age to age.

For some this isn't enough.
They even hear the pouring rain,
they feel the cool drops on necks and shoulders,
they look at the bridge and the people
as if they saw themselves there
in the self-same never-finished run
along an endless road eternally to be travelled
and believe in their impudence
that things are really thus.

π

π deserves our full admiration
three point one four one.
All its following digits are also non-recurring,
five nine two because it never ends.
It cannot be grasped *six five three five* at a glance,
eight nine in a calculus
seven nine in imagination,
or even *three two three eight* in a conceit, that is, a comparison
four six with anything else
two six four three in the world.
The longest snake on earth breaks off after several metres.
Likewise, though at greater length, do fabled snakes.
The series comprising π
doesn't stop at the edge of the sheet,
it can stretch across the table, through the air,
through the wall, leaf, bird's nest, clouds, straight to heaven,
through all the heavens' chasms and distensions.

How short, how mouse-like, is the comet's tail!
How frail a star's ray, that it bends in any bit of space!
Meanwhile, *two three fifteen three hundred nineteen*
my telephone number the size of your shirt
the year *nineteen hundred and seventy three sixth* floor
the number of inhabitants *sixty-five* pennies
the waist measurement *two* fingers a charade a code,
in which *singing still dost soar, and soaring ever singest*
and quiet please
and also heaven and earth shall pass away,
but not π, no, certainly not,
she's still on with her passable *five*
above-average *eight*
the not-final *seven*
urging, yes, urging a sluggish eternity
to persevere.

Utopia

An island where everything becomes clear.

Here one can stand on the ground of proofs.

The only road has its destination.

Shrubs are burdened with answers.

Here grows the tree of Proper Conjecture,
its branches eternally untangled.

The dazzlingly straight tree of Understanding
is next to a spring called Ah So That's How It Is.

The deeper you're in the wood, the wider grows
the Valley of Obviousness.

Whatever the doubt, the wind blows it away.

Echo speaks uncalled
and readily solves the mysteries of worlds.

On the right a cave where sense reclines.

To the left a lake of Deep Conviction.
Truth stirs from the bottom and lightly breaks the surface.

Unshakeable Certainty dominates the vale
and Essence of Things spreads from its head.

Despite these attractions, the island is deserted,
and the tiny footmarks seen along the shores
all point towards the sea.

As though people always went away from here
and irreversibly plunged into the deep.

In life that's inconceivable.

Unwritten poem reviewed

In the opening words of her composition
the author asserts that the Earth is small,
while the sky is unconscionably vast
and, I quote, 'contains more than necessary' stars.

In her description of the heavens one detects a certain helplessness,
the author loses herself in the terrible void,
she is struck by the lifelessness of many planets
and presently her mind (which lacks rigour)
poses the question
whether, after all, we are alone
under the sun, under all the suns of the universe.

Flouting the calculus of probability!
And all the generally accepted convictions!
Despite incontrovertible proof which any day now
may fall into our hands! Ah, well, poetry.

Meanwhile, our oracle returns to Earth,
a planet which perhaps 'rolls on without witnesses',
the sole 'science-fiction the cosmos can afford'.
The despair of Pascal (1623-1662 [ed.])
appears to the author to have no match
on Andromeda or Cassiopeia.
Uniqueness exaggerates and obligates,
and thus arises the problem of how to live, and so on,
since 'emptiness will not resolve that for us'.
'My God, man cries to His Own Self,
have mercy on me, bring me light...'

The author is haunted by the thought of life so effortlessly frittered away,
as though there were endless supplies of it;
by wars which – according to her perverse opinion –
are always lost on both sides;
by man's 'depopulation' (*sic!*) of man.
A moral intent flickers in the work
and would probably have glowed under a less naïve pen.

A pity, though. This fundamentally risky thesis
(are we after all perhaps alone
beneath the sun, beneath all the suns of the universe)
and its development in her happy-go-lucky style
(a mixture of loftiness and common speech)
causes us to ask whether anyone would believe it.
No one surely. Quite so.

ZBIGNIEW HERBERT

Even after the award of the Nobel prize to Miłosz, **Zbigniew Herbert** remains the most celebrated Polish poet in the West, and, remarkable for a country whose poetry reaches back into the Middle Ages, perhaps the *first* Polish poet the West has taken at all seriously.

Herbert was born in 1924. He fought in the Resistance and after the war attended academic institutions in Toruń, Kraków and Warsaw, gaining degrees in law, commerce and philosophy. During the Stalinist years he held various undistinguished jobs and his first volume of poetry was not published until 1956. His *Collected Poems* first appeared in 1971 and an enlarged edition in 1982; he has also written radio plays and essays in art history. His most recent book is *Report from the Besieged City and other poems*, published in Paris in 1983 and in English (translated by John and Bogdana Carpenter) by Oxford University Press in 1987.

MAREK ORAMUS: Are you aware of the fact that in Poland you practically don't exist ? I've been to a public library and haven't found any of your books. It's a long time since your works appeared in bookshops, and your plays are not being staged. You are frequently published abroad where you enjoy greater popularity than in your own country. I hear there are Mr Cogito clubs in America.
HERBERT: There is a periodical in America called *Mr Cogito*, but I haven't heard of any clubs. You must have confused me with *Playboy*. I know I do not exist in Poland but I cannot help it. I don't plead with publishers or cultural policy-makers. They know, or at least should know, what they are doing... The language of politics and literature are entirely different and so are the mentalities. Politicians are concerned with "far-reaching" goals, personal games, gangster-style tricks. What interests me is human fate. What does me good is bad for politicians: what suits them I find indigestible. We use two separate styles. I have tried to use the conditional. I hesitate, I appeal to conscience. I dislike the imperative, exclamation mark, black and white divisions.
ORAMUS: In your poems you write about your native Lwów.
HERBERT: Lwów used to be a centre for humanists and scholars; father would recite the *Odyssey* to me when I was three. There was no need to look up the word *polis* in the dictionary. It was obvious. I was growing up in it.
ORAMUS: My hypothesis is that you like history because you are dissatisfied with reality.
HERBERT: A very pertinent question. But you see – all my life, and I am nearly sixty, I have virtually stayed in one place and yet my citizenship has changed four times. I was a citizen in pre-war Poland,

the Second Commonwealth; then Lwów was annexed to West
Ukraine, there is still a note in my passport stating that I was born
in the USSR; then I became a *Kennkarte* citizen in the German
Government General and eventually I came to live in People's
Poland. I have lived through four distinct political systems. This
specific condensation is responsible for my sense of history – some
kind of empathy, an ability to understand people of distant epochs.
ORAMUS: Now that you are back, are you going to stay for some time?
HERBERT: I think I am. I was going to remain abroad for another
year because it suited my literary arrangements. I couldn't bear the
pressure of information, or rather pseudo-information, and specu-
lation about the events in Poland. At a distance of six hundred or
some six thousand kilometres from Warsaw, Polish problems, the
problems that have always been the most important for me, begin
to reach monstrous proportions. In our emotional space, distance,
unlike in geometry, makes things grow immensely large.
[Warsaw, April 1981]

'Unlike the more direct Różewicz...Herbert is primarily an ironic
re-interpreter of myths and literary themes as a way of illuminating
and containing the emotional, moral and intellectual dilemmas, and
the tragic or deeply unnerving experiences of the post-war Polish
poet.

'Herbert is also exceptional among the post-war poets writing in
Poland in that he succeeded in reconstructing fully the function of
the poet as the renovator and creator of values, in addition to his
function as a critic of ideologies, systems and conventions. In fact,
his poetry combines the two functions in a manner that strengthens
them both.

'Herbert's poetry has been called classical, and the description is
not only justified but very apt. Operating within poetic conventions,
Herbert uses them to reveal tension, but while revealing it, he also
controls it by means of the same conventions, hence the richness
and subtlety of the semantic aspect of his poems and their ironic
mode. Similarly, his use of myths and archetypes, cultural and liter-
ary allusions and *loci communes* is double-edged, for these intelli-
gences from the past not only illumine modern predicaments, but
are themselves revitalised and often re-interpreted.' (Bogdan
Czaykowski)

The story of the Minotaur

The real story of prince Minotaur is told in the as yet undeciphered linear script A. Contrary to later gossip, he was the true son of king Minos and of Pasiphaë. The boy was born with an abnormally large head, a sign, according to soothsayers, of future wisdom. In fact Minotaur grew into a strong somewhat morose cretin. The king decided to enter him for the priesthood. But the priests argued that they couldn't accept the abnormal prince for fear of lowering the authority of religion already shaken by the invention of the wheel.

So Minos brought over Daedalus who was fashionable in Greece as the pioneer of the well-known Pedagogic Movement in architecture. And that is how the labyrinth came about. By means of a system of passages, ranging from the simplest to the most complex, of various levels and steps of abstraction, it was to instil in the prince the laws of ordered thought.

So, prodded by tutors, the luckless prince meandered through passages of induction and deduction, staring wildly at ideological frescoes. He understood nothing.

Having exhausted all possible means, king Minos decided to get rid of this disgrace to his line. He brought (again from Greece which had a reputation for clever people) a deft assassin named Theseus. And Theseus killed Minotaur. At this point myth and history are in accord.

Theseus returns through the labyrinth, now a useless primer, carrying Minotaur's huge bloody head with bulging eyes that for the first time sprout wisdom commonly bestowed by experience.

Why the classics
(for A.H.)

1

in the fourth book of *The Peloponesian War*
Thucydides describes his unsuccessful expedition

amid long speeches by generals
sieges battles disease
thick webs of intrigue
diplomatic demarches
that episode is like a needle
in a forest

the Athenian colony Amphipolis
fell to Brasydas
because Thucydides' relief was late

for this he paid with life-long exile
from his native city

exiles of all time
know that price

2

the generals in recent wars
in similar predicaments
yap on their knees before posterity
praise their own heroism
and innocence

they blame subordinates
envious colleagues
and hostile winds

Thucydides merely says
it was winter
he had seven ships
had sailed at speed

3
should the theme of art
be a broken jug
a tiny broken soul
full of self-pity

then what shall remain of us
will be like lovers' tears
in a dingy small hotel
when wallpapers dawn

Curatia Dionisia

The stone is well preserved   The inscription (corrupt Latin)
proclaims that Curatia Dionisia lived forty years
and at her own expense had raised this modest little monument
Lonely is her banquet   The cup half-drained
Unsmiling face   Doves too ponderous
Her last years she spent in Britain
by the wall of the halted barbarians
in a castrum of which the foundations and cellars remain

She practised woman's oldest profession
She was mourned briefly but sincerely by the soldiers of the Third
      Legion
and a certain aged officer

She instructed the sculptors to place two pillows under her elbow

Dolphins and sea-lions signify a long journey
even though from here it's just a step to hell

Pan Cogito on virtue

1

It's not surprising
she is not the bride
of real men

generals
strongmen
despots

they are followed down the ages
by that weepy old maid
in a terrible Salvation Army bonnet
who nags

she fetches a portrait of Socrates
from an old lumber-room
a cross kneaded in bread
old words

– while all around a splendid life roars
pink like an abattoir at dawn

one could almost bury her
in a silver casket
of innocent souvenirs

she shrinks
like hair in the throat
like a buzz in the ear

2

My God
if only she were a little younger
and prettier

marched with the spirit of the times
swung her hips
to the beat of fashionable music

perhaps real men would then
fall in love with her
generals strongmen despots

if only she took more care
looked human
like Liz Taylor
or the Goddess of Victory

but she stinks of
mothballs
her lips are sealed
she reiterates the great No

insufferably stubborn
comic like a scarecrow
like an anarchist's dream
like the lives of saints

Report from Paradise

In paradise a working week lasts thirty hours
wages are higher prices fall
physical toil does not tire (due to weaker gravity)
wood chopping is no worse than typing
the social structure is stable and those in authority wise
honestly in paradise things are better than anywhere

At first it was to be different –
luminous circles choirs stages of abstraction
but it proved impossible to divide exactly
body from soul which would arrive here
trailing a drop of lard a thread of muscle
the conclusion had to be drawn
a grain of the absolute had to be mixed with a grain of clay
one more departure from doctrine the last departure
John alone had foreseen this: ye shall rise in the flesh

Only a few behold God
he is for those of pure pneuma
the rest listen to communiques about miracles and floods
in time all shall behold God
when this will be no one knows

Meanwhile on Saturdays at noon
sirens bray sweetly
heavenly proletarians emerge from factories
carrying their wings clumsily like violins under their arms

Pan Cogito's soul

In the past
we know from history
she left the body
when the heart stopped

with the last breath
she departed quietly
for heavenly meadows

    Pan Cogito's soul
    behaves differently

    in his life-time she leaves his body
    without a goodbye

    months years she spends
    on other continents
    beyond Pan Cogito's boundaries

    it's hard to find her address
    she sends no news
    avoids contact
    doesn't write letters

    no one knows when she'll be back
    perhaps she's gone for good

Pan Cogito tries to overcome
a base feeling of jealousy

thinks well of the soul
thinks of the soul tenderly

doubtless she has to dwell
in other bodies too

decidedly there are not enough souls
for the whole of humanity

Pan Cogito accepts fate
he has no other option

even tries to say
'my soul mine'

he thinks of his soul lovingly
he thinks of his soul tenderly

　　so when she appears
　　unexpectedly
　　he doesn't greet her with
　　'it's good you're back'

　　he only looks askance
　　when she sits facing a mirror
　　when she combs her
　　tangled white hair

Pan Cogito's thoughts on Hell

Contrary to popular belief, the lowest circle of hell is not inhabited
either by despots, matricides or those who are seekers after flesh.
It is a refuge for artists, full of mirrors, pictures and instruments.
To a casual observer, the most comfortable infernal department
without brimstone, tar or physical torture.

All the year round there are competitions, festivals and concerts.

There is no high season. The season is permanent and almost absolute. Every quarter new Movements spring up and nothing, it appears, can arrest the triumphal procession of the Avantgarde.

Beelzebub loves art. He boasts that his choirs, poets and painters almost outstrip the celestials. Better art means better government – that's obvious. Soon they will be able to test their strengths at the Two Worlds Festival. Then we'll see if Dante, Fra Angelico and Bach make the grade.

Beelzebub supports art. His artists are guaranteed peace, good food and total isolation from infernal life.

Old Masters

The Old Masters
dispensed with names

their signatures
were the white fingers of the Madonna

or pink towers
di citta sul mare

and also scenes from the life
della Beata Umiltà

they dissolved
in sogno
miracolo
crocifissione

they found refuge
under an angel's eyelid
behind hillocks of clouds
in the thick grasses of paradise

they drowned totally
in golden sunsets
without cries of terror
or pleas for remembrance

the surfaces of their paintings
are smooth like mirrors

mirrors not for us
mirrors for the elect

I call upon you Old Masters
in moments of deep despair

cause me to shed
the snake skin of pride

may I remain deaf
to temptations of fame

I call upon you Old Masters

Painter of Manna Rain
Painter of Embroidered Towers
Painter of the Visitation
Painter of the Sacred Blood

Prayer of Pan Cogito – Traveller

Lord
>   thank you for creating the world beautiful and of such variety

>   and also for allowing me in your inexhaustible goodness
>   to visit places which were not the scene of my daily torments

>   – for lying at night near a well in a square in Tarquinia while
>   the swaying
>   bronze declared from the tower your wrath and forgiveness

and a little donkey on the island of Corcyra sang to me from its incredible bellowing lungs the landscape's melancholy

and in the very ugly city of Manchester I came across very good and sensible people

nature reiterated her wise tautologies the forest was forest the sea was sea and rock was rock

stars orbited and things were as they should be – Jovis omnia plena

– forgive me for thinking only of myself when the life of others cruel and irreversible turned round me like the huge astrological clock in the church at Beauvais

for being too cowardly and stupid because I did not understand so many things

and also forgive me for not fighting for the happiness of poor and vanquished nations and for seeing only moonrise and museums
– thank you for the works created to glorify you which have shared with me part of their mystery so that in gross conceit

I concluded that Duccio Van Eyck Bellini painted for me too

and likewise the Acropolis which I had never fully understood patiently revealed to me its mutilated flesh

– I pray that you do not forget to reward the white-haired old man who brought me fruit from his garden in the bay of the island of Ithaca

and also the teacher Miss Hellen on the isle of Mull whose hospitality was Greek or Christian and who ordered light to be placed in the window facing Holy Iona so that human lights might greet one another

and furthermore all those who had shown me the way and said *kato kyrie kato*

and that you should have in your care the Mother from Spoleto
Spiridion from Paxos and the good student from Berlin who
got me out of a tight spot and later, when I unexpectedly
ran into him in Arizona, drove me to Grand Canyon which
is like a hundred thousand cathedrals standing on their heads

   – grant O Lord that I may forget my foolish and very weary
   persecutors when the sun sets into the vast uncharted
   Ionian sea

   that I may comprehend other men other tongues other suffering
   and that I be not stubborn because my limitations are
   without limits

   and above all that I be humble, that is, one who sees
   one who drinks at the spring

   thank you O Lord for creating a world very beautiful and varied

   and if this is Your temptation I am tempted for ever
   and without forgiveness

The power of taste
(for Prof. Izydora Dąbska)*

No our refusal dissent and obduracy
didn't require great character
we had a pinch of indispensable courage
but basically it was a matter of taste
                Yes taste
containing fibres of soul and gristle of conscience

---

* Izydora Dąbska died in 1983. In an obituary notice, the Warsaw monthly
Twórczość wrote: 'All Poland knew of her, even though twice (in Warsaw
and Kraków) she had been forbidden to lecture, even though some of her
books like *Two Studies of Plato* and *French 16th and 17th Century Scepticism*,
had to wait nearly twenty years for publication. She had offers to teach
abroad but refused them because she felt needed here – and she was right…
It is good to know that the already famous, but [in Poland] as yet unpublished
poem [by Zbigniew Herbert] on the question of taste bears a dedication to
her.' [Ed.]

Who knows had they tempted us more cleverly and beautifully
sent pink wafer-thin flat women
or fantastic creatures by Hieronymus Bosch
but in fact what was hell like in those days
a damp ditch murderers' alley a shack
christened the palace of justice
a do-it-yourself Mephisto in a Lenin jacket
despatched missions made up of the *Aurora's* grandchildren
boys with ashen-grey faces
and very ugly girls with red hands

Indeed their rhetoric was too coarse-grained
(Mark Tully was turning in his grave)
chains of tautologies one or two concepts like flails
a torturer's dialectic no elegance in argument
a syntax lacking the charms of the conditional

Thus therefore aesthetics may be useful in life
one mustn't neglect the study of beauty

Before we join we have scrupulously to examine
the shape of architecture the rhythm of fifes and drums
the official colours and the villainous ritual of funerals

    Our eyes and ears refused obedience
    the princes of our senses chose proud exile

No that didn't require great character
we had a pinch of indispensable courage
but basically it was a matter of taste
                Yes taste
which makes one withdraw squirm or hiss out derision
even if this results in the fall of a body's priceless capital – its head

Our child

Our test-tube baby is developing splendidly
the blue-eyed infant pinky Futurus
was spared measles whooping cough and fever
bed-wetting and the fear of witches and gremlins
he loved UFOs which gave him friendly winks

When he was three he succumbed to senile dementia
so they changed his head in the plant
where he saw the light of day he returned soon
to play audibly with his robot in our sitting room

A penetrating analyst took an interest in his soul
(or rather in that hole Plato called the soul)
our son's IQ upset all known statistics
and the child soon became a tests champion
being well-off we didn't insist he join a circus
after all he is our child as well as the test-tube's
just one TV performance that's all

As clever as young Pascal epoch-making like Einstein
doesn't go to school in case he develops complexes
studies on his own writes and listens to oriental music
which allows him to penetrate supra-rational nexuses

When he was twelve he published books
which entered best-seller lists
reviewers praised the excellent syntheses
he compared Marx with Buddha Christ with Talleyrand
some maliciously blamed him for conceptual muddles
even though our son had freed himself from concepts

But it does bother us that he tends to be gloomy
and often gets very irritable
there are words and phrases you can't use in his presence

such as God conscience and nation
he stamps his feet and stops his ears
but unfailingly he enjoys funerals
wars plagues famines revolutions

Our test-tube son will become a professor
he waits for them to open a suitable department
he's working on a system called Presentism
which boldly rejects all ontology
the mouldy categories of space and time
and a few other details

                          simplifying a great deal
it's the philosophy of the moment of events
unconnected either with the cosmos or with each other
an apologia that is for absolute freedom

when one void sends out flashing signals
while another responds with a hearty laugh

Pan Cogito: the return

    1
Pan Cogito
decided to return
to the stony bosom
of his native land

it is a dramatic decision
he will bitterly regret

but he can no longer
bear the colloquial expressions
'comment allez-vous'
'wie geht's'
'how are you'

the apparently simple questions
demand a convoluted reply

Pan Cogito tears off
the bandages of sympathetic indifference

he no longer believes in progress
he's concerned with his own wound

shop-windows of plenty
fill him with boredom

all he's become attached to are
a Doric column in
the church of San Clemente
a portrait of a certain lady
a book he's had no time to read
and a few other odds and ends

and so he is returning

he sees
the border
the ploughed field

murderous sentry-towers
the thick vegetation of barbed wire
silent
armour-plated doors
slowly close behind him

and now
he is alone
in a treasure-house
of all misfortunes

2
so his friends
from the better world
ask why he is returning
he could have stayed here
tried to settle down

trusted his wound
to chemical stain-removers
left it in a deposit-box
in some huge airport

so why is he returning

'to the waters of childhood'
'to twisted roots'
'to a hand a face
burnt on the grid-iron of time'

apparently simple questions
demand a convoluted reply

maybe Pan Cogito is returning
to give a reply

to the whispers of fear
to impossible happiness
to a sudden blow
to a killing question

Pan Cogito on the need for rigour

1
Pan Cogito
is worried by a problem
in applied mathematics

the difficulties we encounter
in simple arithmetical operations

children are lucky
they add apple to apple
subtract seed from seed
the answer is correct
the playschool of the world
pulsates with assuring warmth

we now have the measurements of elementary particles
the weight of heavenly bodies
and only in human affairs
culpable negligence
and a lack of precise detail proliferate

spectral indeterminacy
haunts the boundlessness of history

how many Greeks perished near Troy
– we don't know

let's have the precise losses
on both sides
in the battle of Gaugamela
Agincourt
Leipzig
Kutno

also how many victims of
white
red
and brown
terror
(those colours innocent colours)

– we don't know
we really don't know

Pan Cogito
rejects the reasonable explanation
that it all happened long ago
the wind had mixed the ashes
the blood had drained into the sea

reasonable explanations
increase
Pan Cogito's anxiety

for even
what occurs under our gaze
slips beyond numbers
loses the human dimension

somewhere there must be a fault
a fatal failure of instruments
or a sin of memory

2
a few simple examples
of the calculus of victims

it's easy to establish
the exact number of the dead
in an aircrash

that is important for beneficiaries
and life offices
plunged in grief

we pick up the list of passengers
and crew
place a cross
against each name

it's a little bit
more difficult
when trains crash

one has to fit together
torn bodies
lest any head
be left unclaimed

during natural disasters
the calculus
becomes
involved

we count the survivors
while the unknown remainder
which is neither alive
nor definitely dead
we define curiously
as missing

they still have a chance
to return to us
from fire
water
the bowels of the earth

if they return – that's fine
if they don't – bad luck

3

Now Pan Cogito
ascends
to the highest rickety
level of indeterminacy

how difficult it is to establish the names
of all those who perished
in conflicts with inhuman rule

official statistics
diminish their number
once more mercilessly
decimate the fallen

and their bodies vanish
in abysmal cellars
of huge police buildings

eye-witnesses
blinded by gas
deafened by salvoes
fear and despair
tend to exaggerate

bystanders
provide questionable figures
qualified with the shameful
little word "approximately"

but surely in these matters
accuracy is essential
we can't be mistaken
even by one

despite everything
we are our brothers' keepers

ignorance about the missing
unhinges the reality of the world

it hurls us into a hell of appearances
a devilish net of a dialectic
which proclaims there's no difference
between substance and spectre

    So we need to know
    to count accurately
    call by name
    provide for the journey

    millet and poppy-seed
    in a clay dish
    a bone comb
    arrow-heads
    a loyalty ring

    amulets

The Passion of Our Lord painted by an anonymous hand from the Circle of Rhenish Masters

They have coarse features, their hands are deft and accustomed to a hammer and nails, to wood and iron. Just now they are nailing to the cross Jesus Christ Our Lord. There's lots to be done, they must hurry to get things ready by noon.

Knights on horseback – they are the props of this drama. Impassive faces. Long lances imitate trees without branches on this hillock without trees.

As we said, the fine craftsmen are nailing Our Lord to the cross. Ropes, nails, and a stone for sharpening the tools, are ranged neatly on the sand. There's a hum of activity but without due excitement.

The sand is warm, each grain painstakingly depicted. Here and there a tuft of stiffly erect grass and a marguerite innocently white cheering the eye.

JAN DAROWSKI

Jan Darowski was born in 1926 in Silesia and attended a printing college in Katowice. In 1944 he was press-ganged into the German Army. During the Normandy campaign he crossed to the Allied side and joined the Polish Armoured Division. After the War he settled in London.

Is writing poetry a life-time commitment? In many cases it turns out to be a youthful passion and, if that would have been the case with Keats, Trakl, Owen, Bursa and Wojaczek, their early deaths have not, contrary to common assumption, deprived us of poetic masterpieces. But they may have persevered and even, like Mickiewicz, Norwid, Hopkins and Yeats, moved in new directions in middle age. Generalisations prove unhelpful, particularly when someone, like Darowski, produces a slim first volume at the age of 43, and then shortly afterwards, like a middle-aged Rimbaud, renounces and denounces the whole enterprise.

Darowski is also an acute literary critic. Long residence outside Poland and considerable experience as translator has made him especially sensitive to the way in which language moulds consciousness, and he has in a series of provocative and incisive essays blamed the woolliness of Polish writers and intellectuals on the miasmas of the Polish language.

'The title of the volume, *Drzewo sprzeczki (The Tree of Contention),**
is apt: Darowski's poems are, with few exceptions, witty and often angry reflections upon various aspects of modern society and civilisation. His language is highly functional, heated, argumentative, punning and firmly rooted in personal experience. At the same time he shows marked affinities with several post-war Polish poets (especially Karpowicz) and, among English poets, with D.H. Lawrence whom he has translated into Polish...An example of Darowski's style at its best is the poem 'The Way'. It is more compact than some of his poems, free of gratuitous punning, bitterly outspoken and sarcastic rather than ironic.' (Bogdan Czaykowski)

---

* I prefer *'The Querulous Tree'* [Ed.]

Post-mortem

With the star of David they vanished beneath our earth,
they poisoned the air with dioxide of deadly psalms –
we too must suffocate, we, the murder's witnesses,
and with the torturer hand in hand march bowed through history.

Alcohol will not help. Our oily purple
hypocrisy floats to the surface.
Monuments are no use, no use saying we were like them
defenceless. Not everyone regretted
the sword cutting our Gordian knot,
cutting the nation's twin life.
Alcohol's no use – Lethe of cowards and fools.

The killer may offer his white-gloved
hand to those that survived,
may say – look, my right hand
is clean and unaware
of what the other hand did.

While a pensive righteous Christian
dropping cigar ash into the Atlantic
may say – true, the inscription was there
and so was my hand
but I had left my glasses behind.

In this conspiracy we were the oldest,
not bound by silence even,
we ate common bread, drank
from self-same rock, their hands touched us,
the blood-drained hands of biblical tailors –
– –
Those same hands are wind against the pane
shake the wreath's red shame
                                shake the memory.

Life

They – enchanted
he – disenchanted

Together they played under the table
learnt to walk
time ran they ran carefree like kids
for them the cuckoo was the clock,
the tin weathercock in charge of winds
the highest church dignitary

The same sun rose for them each morning
through the pear tree in rays of poetry
the same heart set beyond the forest
eyes beyond mists, hands in mother's hair,
they would return from mountain excursions
unearthily withdrawn
carrying the July night on their backs like enormous wings
in the same wintry moon they dipped their pens
to describe death

And here life divided them

they still see
a birch skeleton on a hill with a red apple
in cool veils of mist,
he sees a glowing plain
on which his trembling hand plants a row of crosses –
like an illiterate
signing a document he doesn't understand

The Way

When man loses himself
he begins to search for a roundabout way to the Indies
or the moon
or socialism
cuts down trees, heads, pours concrete everywhere
lays paving stones, erects street-lights and signs

But Holy Jerusalem, the city of the Covenant,
has vanished beyond the forests,
they have drained away the rainbow
when they drained the swamps

Animals fear us,
neither flowers nor God
now wish to speak to us –
when we open our mouths
we spew stones
what is man to make of them?
He builds a house
a tower of babble, a prison, a tombstone –
kneeling in a field, his back to the sun
wiping cold sweat from his brow
he constructs
his highway from nowhere to nowhere

WIKTOR WOROSZYLSKI

Wiktor Woroszylski was born in 1927 in Grodno (which is now in the Soviet Union) and studied literature in Moscow, Łódź and Warsaw. His *Selected Poems* appeared in 1974 and an enlarged edition in 1982. He has also published various prose works, including a biography of Mayakovsky.

In 1956 Woroszylski was editor of *Nowa Kultura*, the leading communist literary weekly and was full of trust in the new system. But during the turmoil in Poland and Hungary he became celebrated for his Budapest despatches on the Hungarian uprising published in *Nowa Kultura*. In the late 70s he became editor of the leading dissident periodical *Zapis*. In 1982 he was interned under martial law for his agitation in the Ursus vehicle plant in Warsaw.

At his best, Woroszylski displays the irony, subtlety, allusiveness and understanding that one associates with Miłosz and Herbert. His collection *Zagłada gatunków (Extermination of the species)*, published in 1970, well illustrates these admirable qualities. At a time when, revolted by ideological dogmatism, the young were discovering the early Marx and calling for socialism with a human face, Woroszylski rather perversely still tried to discover these very qualities in the old man:

> I am intrigued by and drawn to the Old Marx not so
> violent and dramatic as the Young Marx nor so
> biting More difficult...
> I trust the Old Marx who
> of course wants to change the world but also
> wants to understand it

Thus, while at odds with the actual embodiment of communist rule in Poland at the present time, Woroszylski, unlike, say, Herbert, remains committed to the left, and his reflections on the totalitarian forces of our time are usually very general and allegorical as in 'Filatelistyka' ('Philately'):

> I recall
> the philately of my childhood   Who's noticed
> that the philately of our childhood
> has disappeared...
>   Resourcefulness
> imagination phantasy all these
> made up an open world which I am today
> ashamed to long for unsure of
> my present motives now when
> there is a different philately of
> closed systems...
>   There is
> organisation and specialisation these powers
> of the modern world   The total
> philately

or in 'Franz Kafka', where the poet insists that the author of *The Trial* 'lived in the mildest tyranny of all' and that only later did Europe come to embody his nightmarish vision. And when he does become a little more specific, it is to speculate on the nature of 'Fascist nations' born in Europe after World War I, and he notes the banality of this particular type of evil, unheralded by comets and evolving quietly amidst 'ordinary folk and good folk', and people 'who knew nothing'.

Myth about mass culture

Time devoured the fish
Its shadow's impressed upon stone
But who prayed to the fish time swallowed
A shaggy one peered from behind a rock
Not aware of time he feared thunder
Skies cracked
Thunder was the speech of time
Time was deadly fear
Gods appeared in the cleft

It was they who defended man
Extracted immortality from a fetid corpse
Placed it in a rosy shroud
Led it into lands where time did not kill
Death was metaphor and metamorphosis
Shades played upon zithers
Grateful man raised fanes
Now fully armed he peered from behind the rock

Time devoured the Gods
Ore was smelted into crowns of another shape
Iron cable cut marble columns
Stones were scattered stone was placed upon stone
A powerful God would snatch lambs from a weaker deity
Would turn back processions
Would alter the wailing note
Would crush yesterday's colours
Would sink into time

Cultural history is more precise
It reveals layers of Gods
Orders them into a relay race and plugs in a chronometer
Which lacks the needle of fear
Mutability grows statuesque in museums

So now we witness the phase of Esso Shell Mobiloil Gods
Oil is flowing on the altars of speed
Nickelodeons grind time
Shades of gladiators and crusaders are cast on cinemascope

Ruins of ancient cultures with guides souvenirs pedlars
   learned authors of prospectuses have been hired to while
   away the time of worshippers on their way to the
   petrol and coca-cola soaked temples of the new cult of
   the universal people-unifying mass culture
Who peers from behind the rock
It's us tourists
We're returning to the catacombs with cameras
Before thunder strikes
And our shade is impressed upon stone

Delegation

This was an official trip concerning poetry
to a town in which I had once been much younger
on another occasion I merely felt younger and
this still roused certain hopes but this journey
was a tribute to my and my four colleagues'
competence on the subject of poetry we were that is
to choose winners of a competition hand them each a rose we had to
   read
four hundred poems we had already read more written more
we had received and had not received roses our roses withered
they now expected us to know what poetry is in the cosy
compartment we discussed the new fashion in hats and
the civilisation of the Incas destroyed by the conquistadors which
according to some amongst us wasn't as perfect as is supposed it knew
slavery torture mental illness we travelled
through a muddied evening from which suddenly
a stone detached itself broke the window showering us
with splintered glass in our hair on our suits
one of us had a cut on his cheek the guard shook
his head these pranks on the line while they were clearing up
we went to the dining car after we paid the bill
we found we were done out of fifty
zlotys so one of us got up shyly did not want to
with the waiter but another got up and cried waiter
who returned the cash making excuses so we reached
the dais where we handed out roses to the deeply
moved victors the first brought along his old

mousey mother she made gestures of supplication such triumph
    another
flew down from the hills a sportsman swift and accurate he abandoned
that whirring plane the third was a clown
thanked for the serious consideration later
we went to the hotel and there were no incidents
and yet it all seemed an adventure because
it happened in a strange place beyond the day's routine
of arrival and departure when the following day
we met students a little fairhaired chap
asked whom he should flatter in order to get
his poems published it wasn't a cynical question he
was concerned with technique of a profession more elusive
than engineering we drank vodka slept
in chilly hotel-beds the receptionist was rude we resolved
to stay calm there were no incidents did I
want adventure I had first symptoms of 'flu we returned
from our official trip at dawn rain washed the panes
of telephone booths trams croaked – what then
is poetry
               Discussion of ancient civilisation or
a stone which cuts it short feeling shame for someone who
tried to cheat us or exacting
what is due momentary withdrawal
from daily routine by a change of place an escape or return at dawn
denial or triumph all these contrasts
are incidental and arise directly
out of the happenings of those few days which after all
could have been quite different prompting also different
ideas and definitions equally good or equally bad what then
is poetry which I then felt so tangibly
and vividly what then is what then is poetry is it in
what I described to you at length will you accept it or will you
demand various operations for which
I have neither energy nor strength because the last thing
I believe is that poetry resides in poeticising operations is there
anyone competent or did I accept those 500 zlotys
unlawfully for judging if I do not know
what poetry is and the return of my travelling expenses
of my official trip concerning poetry

ANDRZEJ BURSA

Andrzej Bursa was born in 1932 in Kraków. He began a course in journalism at Kraków University but found the political pressures in the department too oppressive and switched to Slavonic studies. He then worked as a reporter on a Kraków paper.

Bursa died of a heart disease in 1957 and his *Poems* appeared posthumously in 1958. A more substantial *Poetry and Prose*, incorporating previously uncollected and previously unpublished pieces, appeared in 1969 with a third printing in 1982.

'A late autumn evening. It's cold and it's raining. It's a time when you want to get home as quickly as possible. But suddenly his familiar silhouette appears: a black anorak, thick black hair.

"Come with me," he says.

We move off. He is lively, probing, tries to pierce me right through, while I am wet and puzzled. I deliberately stay silent, waiting for an explanation of the important reason which compels us to promenade in the rain.

"Why is it so difficult to be famous today?" Andrzej Bursa resumes his favourite monologue. "Take Byron, Mickiewicz, Rimbaud, Pushkin – they were so young when they became famous throughout

Europe. And us? Nobody knows us apart from a couple of editors. We crawl on the ground: advances and fees to save us from starving, begging for publication, rows with censors. Always on our knees. Have you noticed that people of our generation are kneeling almost all the time? Parents, teachers, employers, friends – they all demand the same ritual. After all, I am quite old, I'm twenty."' (Stanisław Stanuch)

'His is a poetry of total disenchantment and his desolate, though outwardly tough voice, was instantly recognised by his young contemporaries as the most authentic one in the physical and spiritual desolation wrought by the war and the Stalinist terror.' (Jan Darowski)

Talking to a poet

How to convey scent in poetry...
certainly not through simple naming
scent must permeate the whole
both rhyme
and rhythm
must have the temperature of a honeyed glade
each rhythmical leap
resemble the swaying of a rose
poised over a trellis

we conversed in an atmosphere of the best symbiosis
until I said:
'please remove this bucket
the piss-stench is intolerable'

maybe this was tactless
but I couldn't stand it any longer.

Saint Joseph

Of all Catholic saints
I like Saint Joseph best
he was no masochist
or some other queer
but a professional
always with that axe
without the axe he must have felt
his arm was crippled
and though it came hard to him
he brought up the Brat
which he knew
was not his son
but God's
or somebody else's
and when they were running away from the police
in the night

amid the figured landscapes of Rameses' inhuman architecture
(I suppose that's why "pharaoh" means "policeman")*
he carried the Child
and the heaviest basket.

Morning in the park

Each morning when I share my religious exercises with the trees
I see a lone soul with a small suitcase on a secluded bench
I peep inside the suitcase
                              ugh
                              there is a sliced-up baby
discreetly I turn into another path
someone approaches
dragging a bundle
plop...a woman's leg falls out
this is too much
I run away into the furthest corner
where the park adjoins a disused gravel-pit
here the only person I am likely to meet is that bungling accountant
whose hobby is a herbarium
but what is that pacing by his side ?
                                    a horse ?
                                    a dog ?
something smaller than a horse
yet more imposing than a Great Dane
ah...it's a Chimera
the poor old boy
brings his Chimera to graze here in solitude.

Look out, drama !

A small grey man
as grey as Monday following Sunday
grey as a grey mouse in a grey field

---

* It does in Polish slang. [Ed.]

variously assorted
stocked and sold
wholesale
but available in retail trade
as one item
in a great mass
of identical items
a truly expendable item
much more expendable
than the number by which he is known
has flared up into passionate love

BOGDAN CZAYKOWSKI

Bogdan Czaykowski was born in 1932 in Równe, a provincial town in the south-east corner of pre-war Poland. Deported to the Soviet Union in 1940. He reached England in 1948 via Iran and India. He studied history and literature in Dublin and London, and since 1962 has taught Polish history and literature at the University of British Columbia.

He has published four volumes of poetry and his *Selected Poems* appeared in Paris in 1971. With Bolesław Sulik he wrote a detailed sociological study of Poles in Great Britain and with Andrzej Busza published in English translation *Gathering Time: Five Modern Polish Elegies* (1984).

Czaykowski earned a place in Miłosz's *Post-War Polish Poetry* anthology as one of its youngest representatives because, as Miłosz stated in his *History of Polish Literature*, Czaykowski has 'best expressed the predicament of a poet in exile'. The predicament was further explored in a discussion which Czaykowski initiated in 1959 regarding the problems of writing in Polish in a foreign environment.

'A three-fold alienation. Czaykowski knows he doesn't belong to Poland, that he doesn't belong to his adopted country and doesn't belong among the professional emigrés. His situation is therefore unenviable.' (Zygmunt Ławrynowicz)

'History teaches us that writers were most commonly alienated from the society in which they lived. The need to belong is undoubtedly strong in everyone. But equally strong in every writer is the need for solitude... One need not return to Poland, but one can still strive to be a good writer read in Poland.' (Bogdan Czaykowski)

'His poetry, with its rich, exotic imagery and its profound faith in Nature and Man, stands alone and somewhat apart from current fashions. It is the most musical poetry written in the Polish language today.' (Jan Darowski)

Whatever the losses or gains of exile, it is a fact that Czaykowski has found a role for his poetry with its celebrations of paradisal childhood (in India), its concern over the violence of the modern world and its absorption in the richness of the Canadian landscape. He has produced fine translations of Canadian poetry.

Garden
(for my mother)

Here, in this garden, there certainly is a man.
But though many eyes are seen, they lack embodiment.
Here, in this garden, perhaps there is a woman:
A ripe breast lies amid glittering leaves.
In the rustling sound there is a child's hearing –
Like a convolvulus climbing over stems of sunflowers.
Stealthily I brush aside grasses at someone's feet,
But still lack courage to raise my eyes:
There stands a nakedness and everything is beautiful.
The garden's green arc took me into a quiet parenthesis
And covered the bright swelling with a banana leaf.
I rest my eyes and merely pluck
The crescent moon's bow-string – an arbitrary line.
I feel so satisfied with my construction in the blue
That the lightness of thought lifts the dome of distance,
Distinguishing a brilliant compass of the sky.
In this garden there certainly is a woman:
A white arm reclines upon an apple-tree,
While above, a fragmentary face still seeks completion
And a man's naked torso emerges amid jasmine flowers.
Rustling in layers of leaves and leaves leaves leaves,
Rustling which kindles into a tall shape of flame
Green sparks of buds. The greenery of grass burns,
Night springs at the moon. A peacock slumbers beneath a star,
The wind gathers rusty silver. A palm whimpers over the wastes.
From a coconut shell a woman who certainly is here
Drinks milk. Her body is gilded
By the irreplaceable sun, then twilight chill combs
And heaps warm hair over her shoulder.
So now I will come closer.

                     Darkness rolls down the leaf.
Here was man – here is the space for a hip
Where now a furrowing wave chases leaves across a lake.
He probably placed these olives in that mouth into which flows
A briny drop – on his brow conceived –
A warm drop of sweat.

So I will now retreat
To measure the cactus shadow with the length of my sleep.
Quieta non movere. Let ants milk greenfly.
An axe clears the garden. But the greenery still burns
And enchanting silences yet haunt the garden
Which once was called – and rightly so – *hortus conclusus*
Or paradise, lost, which here I have described
From memory.

Threnos

I
Fingers grasp the flame
and before he's set alight
he hesitates, alone,
then saves the flame from thought,
it catches and in the square
he blazes like a torch.

II
You wish to know how a man burns?
A poem will not explain.
Put your hands in the flames
hold them for the blink
of a lash-singed eyelid.

Put your hands in the fire
if you're a man.

III
Then you'll understand
that before he fetched the fuel-can
he clasped his head in his hands
and thus he burned, alone
like a man.

IV

Then you'll understand that Jan*
before he came to the square
tested the match
soaked his clothes
shook the proffered hands
quietened someone's cry
and tightly wrapped in his coat
entered the dark not blinking an eye.

V

Put your hands in the flame
if you're a man.

[19 January 1969]

Age de la pierre

In this town they've cleared rubble from squares,
built new homes (you can see for
yourself).
Tidied up cemeteries.
Courts have sentenced both sides.
Later there was amnesty for the murdered
and rehabilitation for the living.
Voluntary outlaws were allowed to return.
But they preferred to hope.
Others were absorbed in profits.
Yet repatriations were secured.
Thus some returned to life.
While others could not face the miracle of Lazarus.
You ask, what vistas emerge?
You will not clear away ruined thoughts, even when raising statues
upon each grave.
Until new men arise.
About whom only this is known
that their inheritance will be a burden.

* Jan Palach burnt himself to death in Prague when Soviet troops put an
end to the Czech Spring of 1968. [Ed.]

ANKA KOWALSKA

Anka Kowalska was born in 1932 in Sosnowiec, in the heartland of the Upper Silesian industrial complex. She studied literature at the Catholic University of Lublin and has published poetry and novels.

Given the tensions and violence that Poles constantly have to endure, it is understandable that unlike, say, the British, they perceive their lives as highly politicised and are therefore eager to see this state of affairs reflected in literature. Not surprisingly, this tempts cohorts of hacks to show their hands in expectation of instant fame.

Good instant committed poetry is rare. The two texts by Kowalska which follow belong, I think, to that category.

Here is Kowalska's account of the circumstances under which they were completed during the bleak months following the collapse of Solidarity:

In the camp for women the prison authorities removed every scribbled note – in accordance with the Internment Decree; most often this was done during searches preceding a transportation. From 13 December 1981 I kept a sort of diary. In order to overcome a sudden but permanent inability to concentrate, I spent several weeks trying to reconstruct 'Reason of state', my last poem. Both my diary and the as yet imperfect version of 'Reason of state' were taken from me during a several-hour search preceding penal transportation from Gołdap to Darłówek. Frequent searches in Darłówek made it impossible for me to retain any extended notes with literary pretensions; in any event, I was being moved about quite frequently to make me think that tomorrow, the day after, or today, I would have to tear up with my own hands whatever I might have managed to write once I broke – with the greatest difficulty – my creative cramp, caused by continued overcrowding and a lack of basic privacy. What could be saved had to be contained on scraps of flimsy paper the size of postage stamps; here the austerity of the poetic form helped.

Hence, instead of a diary – these poems.

Reason of state

1
Apart from children
who are ten today
we were all present there
on somewhat different sides
in different towns
but together

some
amongst us fired from real rifles
and not volleys in salute
but into bodies full of helplessness and despair

that is why some of us have remained on flagstones
staining them terribly
until we were cleared away into hygienic sacks
of impermeable plastic
and deposited stealthily in secret earth-vaults
hygienically covered with quicklime

(this is a civilised way with vampires
which in the past they used to spike
to make them withdraw into the void and cease pestering the living)

some
ran along the streets of seaside towns
naively calling for human life
in this best of worlds best not for us
asking for a hearing in palaces with red flags
in halls raised in marble in our honour
but inhabited by different us

who above all have come to love marble
which so effectively resonated with the slogans in our honour
that they jammed the voices of those
calling for human life and a right to respect

some
our fingers gripping our hair
we listened to the shots aimed at our breasts
in the houses of other towns
alive with our ears glued to hostile transmitters
rasping black on white
instead of melting under Chopin mazurkas
in friendly mass-media
and sipping honey from the shapely lips of Polish announcers
putting us into oblivion
with a hearty goodnight all

some
trembled in fear
that perhaps the delicate fabric of the reason of state got scratched
the reason which feels good only as the legendary sea-monster
which devours everything
from a live shipyard-worker to a mercenary writer

In any event
this reason of state was favoured by all reasons
apart only from reasons of heart and mind

these however
were confined in separate cells
in the prison of the skull and the prison of ribs
from whence they occasionally sent despairing coded signals
to their relatives and friends

they did not reach the other us
who issued the fratricidal order
who knocked out the teeth of Radom workers in Radom streets
and remained unpunished .
and after whom the deluge

2
Together with children
who are ten today
we are all present here
on somewhat different sides
in different towns
but together

we who ordered the killings
we who killed
who faced the bullets
who at night put shoes on the feet of our executed sons
under the shifty gaze of vigilant policemen
who have abandoned our marble halls cracked by earth tremors
who breathed gently on the tissue of reasons of state
who had been the rulers of slaves
who had been the slaves of rulers

we who when ordered would forget
every pool of blood spilled on the pavements of towns and in basement
    cells
who remembered these pools
as though they had trickled out of our own veins
who were honouring them long before
they came to be honoured through statues plaques radio and television
who ordered the arrests of those bearing memorial wreaths
who arrested them and beat them
who were arrested
today we stand beneath the stilled cranes
speechless dignitaries removing crowns hats from our heads
dignitaries in mitres
agents with badges under our lapels
the brothers and mothers of bodies in plastic sacks
and those summoned from once hurriedly dug graves
are amongst us

Amongst us surrounded by allied armies
and beneath the black gaze of gun barrels
stretching to one another suspicious arms
for a suspicious embrace
demanded as always by reason of state

[December 1980 – January 1981]

Madness

How brave our young soldiers
how prettily they warm their hands at fires
which light up my country far and wide
how proudly my tanks turn their guns
toward my enemies in my towns and villages

How numerous are the patrols
in the handsome camouflage of my citizens' militia
how vigilantly they examine the identity of trams buses trains
suitcases bags files pockets and identity cards

How bravely detachments of my armed boys
hidden behind Mars-like masks and shields
conquer week by week
my mines my steelworks my docks

How full are the cellars of my orders
what hubbub in my prisons and detention camps
how skippingly
from one corner of my country to the other
Tsarist sleigh transports carry the slaves from place to place

How effectively my summary my military courts
pronounce sentence after sentence
how eager is my Seym*
how firmly is peace bolstered up by my decrees

How creative is the silence of the police curfew
what salutary ideas and solutions come to me then
how interesting is television news

How properly winter has passed
how orderly is spring forecast
how deeply convinced I am that summer will come in its own time
how fittingly will I design autumn

* Polish parliament. [Ed.]

How inevitable is the change of hate into love
achieved by the descent of my security services
one December night Saturday through Sunday

How directly
how effectively
in such beautiful spectacles
how irreversibly I enter history

[April 1982]

ADAM CZERNIAWSKI

Adam Czerniawski was born in 1934 in Warsaw and left Poland
in 1941. He has lived in Turkey, Palestine, Lebanon, West Germany
and, for the last 30 years, in England, where he studied English
literature and philosophy at London, Sussex and Oxford. His *Selected
Poems 1953-1978* appeared in Poland in 1982.

'Czerniawski was born in Poland and though he has been brought
up in England, he is – in a certain sense of his own choice – an
émigré, that is, a split person. One can see this in his poetry even
in such a seemingly supra-national area as...philosophical problems.
Czerniawski is clearly branded by British linguistic philosophy with
its specific relativism, that is, the sense of the dependence of the
picture of the world upon semantics. He is thus a pupil of a very
good school, but of a school...he thinks one-sided...he is convinced
that the limits of language are *not* the ultimate limits of the world,
that burning cities and human death are not simply 'a problem of
reference', but the rigours of this school he has absorbed prevent
him from throwing himself into an irresponsible "existential" hys-
teria.' (Maciej Broński)

'Czerniawski's latest phase, although it builds on his earlier experi-
ments, constitutes a new departure. It is characterised by a progres-
sive elimination of too obviously grotesque or contrasting effects,
purer diction, and a syntax that unobtrusively integrates complex
poetic statements. The poems of this phase reflect Czerniawski's
growing philosophical interests and are, in fact, an attempt to create
what he himself has called philosophical poetry:
"... *the philosophical poet must both accept and reject logic. In a way which
shows that he is fully aware of the paradox, he must celebrate the unicorn,
the golden mountain and the round square, which have all been justly
banished by logicians to the limbo of the null-class.*"'
(Bogdan Czaykowski)

'In the poem 'World' the poet goes even further than Bishop Berkeley
with *esse est percepi*. The point of departure is, as often with Czerni-
awski, descriptive, sensualist, at times as in a genre picture. But this
time the dream element introduces an atmosphere of strangeness
which is indescribable. The poet dreams in future tense what has
already occurred in the past. Thus "someone will sing the fall of
Troy / someone will bite the apple, paint / the last judgment, smash
all the atoms". Catastrophism in future tense will also destroy the
pastoral-synaesthetic "touching of scent" and "carving of sound".
Our "creation of the world" in a dream is independent of the will,
which commands us to close our eyes – so that mythical and historical

facts should combine dream and reality, past and future, into an unbreakable whole until the moment when the dreamt world falls in ruins – until the moment of "cracks in the skull".' (Alicja Lisiecka)

'The experience of time is dramatised in Czerniawski's poetry, because it is, given the whole complexity of the problem of transience, an experience of ignorance...about himself and the cosmos ...In opposition to the human yearning for identification with a specific cultural milieu, the hero of these poems does not believe in the possibility of assimilation. He carries within ruins of various civilisations, philosophies and epochs. Hence such great mixture in his poetry of arcadian, Babylonian, Judaic, Hellenic and other times aimed at warning man that he ought not to promise himself anything, in particular the retention of his humanity.' (Danuta Künstler)

Fish

he fashioned a poem like a fish
the fish is a symbol of saints
it lives in the depths of secretive seas
and resists massive atmospheric pressures
its presence heralds mysteries
it fell into the nets of mankind
and lies cold on a moist slab
each of its verses has immaculate rhythm
scales of its metaphors glisten in the sun
eyes masked in film live in imagination
and when only the skeleton remains
a white negative of symmetrical pine
words will survive illegibly for ever

[1966]

World

The world began thus: in the morning
I opened my eyes, a square of light in the pane,
roof-slates, garden, a plane
zooms low, the date
is today, inside the picture-frame
a mediaeval town.
I have dreamt the apple tree, the lynx and the moon,
I have dreamt the sea, a winged man drowns,
ruins of Babylon smoulder, horses gallop and snort;
now the sun falls on a bowl of fruit,
I touch its crimson scent.
A damp wind molests the shutter, I dream
a world in which all is possible:
someone will sing the fall of Troy
someone will bite the apple, paint
the last judgment, smash all the atoms.

A dream maybe on a steep bank
of a muddy river. I close
my eyes: cracks in the skull
trace the ruin of a dream-forced world.

[1966]

View of Delft
(for H.K.)

1
there is a view of Delft at the Hague
a panorama of Delft at the Hague
to see Delft
merely climb the stairs
where the Mauritshuis vista is not screened by hills
nor spoilt by spreading chestnut trees

Now the concrete conurbations of glass and steel
have blocked my view of Delft
honest citizens have a roof over their heads
children swing in gardens the ponds teem with fish
but the view of russet Delft brick
the view of Delft's shady canals
the view of Delft's churches
lies veiled
in the Palace of Peace in the museum
I stand cut off from those
    drawbridges
    boats at anchor
    the high-collared children
    and women in clogs

2
He was lucky to have seen Delft
perhaps even today a second-class fare will suffice
but to fix the view not in memory only
there had to be one alive in 1657
who either knew the town since childhood
or having come on business from afar

strolled along the canal's sandy shore
the walls and trees on his right
strolled in fine weather
the previous day the air was sultry
during the night came rain and thunder
now therefore in the cooler air
clouds streak across clear skies
some black bring hail and thunder
on such a day this is the view of Delft
the sun uncertain the walls fitfully dark

3

Many things I have loved
language moving into verse
and the clavichord's lament
journeys on international trains
vistas of wooden hills and still waters
I desired the bright flesh of a girl in Delft
I drank light ale
examined brush strokes through a glass

4

These are the simplest elements
water and bricks clouds and the light of the sun
groups of women children and men
an allegorical interpretation is not required
no need for biographical facts
for the puzzling historical setting
the social system or the economy
I don't know who his wife was
who taught him to paint
I don't know why he found himself in Delft
on a somewhat cloudy day
was it chance
a sudden summons into distant parts
or was it a prearranged ordeal
a citizen's duty a commission of the goldsmiths' guild
and that is not the point

5

Today a sudden mist
has veiled the town the train was late
it grew dark and I lost my way
no one understood me
the last chance had gone

6

It is like the perfect sexual act
or Grelling's paradox
that one who never saw the tawny walls
the roof slates now glinting in sunlight
the barges gliding
through a windy day in spring
should get an impression of Delft
not screened behind a complex of high tension wires
nor even behind a factory of luminous faïence

7

I have seen Delft
    I had waited long
    days passed and years
    I studied learned books
    my daughter read about Babylon
    my son glimpsed the infinity of time
I quarrelled with my wife
I paid my bills
I locked the door
I opened the windows
I ate my lunch I sneezed
but still believed I would see Delft
not in dreams not on postcards not on a screen
that I would see the turrets and forts
    reflected in gently flowing water
I have seen Delft
I beheld Delft
I will describe Delft

8

Leaves smouldering in the city park
chestnuts veiled in a bluish smoke
into the pond by which children play
dives a duck
the flight arrested by outstretched feet
a flutter of wings
now still
she is borne aloft gently flowing water

[1967]

Words
(from a sequence of Commentaries)

After lunch on Saturday 8 May 1971 I drive from Cheltenham to London. The road is empty because the cup-tie at Wembley has already started. The honey waviness of the Cotswolds is moulded by the enamelled sky and dark greenery.

In the morning mother rang to say father probably won't survive the prostate operation. My son wants me to take him along. He is nine. I explain that the sight will not be pleasant and that grandpa in his delirium would not even recognise him.

The last chess game they had together was in December – let that stay in his memory. For the time being I don't realise that doubts as to whether my decision was the right one will haunt me for a long time, especially since father was to regain consciousness that day.

So the landscape is drained of the expected pathos. Instead, it is characterised by crystal clarity in which objects are made to stand out, perceived with an eye focussing with vivid emotions. That is why I am confirmed in my conviction, mistaken as it happens, that I am driving through a countryside which was the inspiration of Samuel Palmer's charmed 'Valley Thick with Corn'.

On the day of the funeral I first have to conduct a seminar on the life and work of Ludwig W. who died just twenty years ago from cancer of the prostate. He often contemplated suicide. He was troubled by the conviction that he was misunderstood, he was horrified at the 'darkness of this time', but at the moment of his death in Cambridge he called out 'Tell them I've had a wonderful life!'

Did he wish to remind us of the words of his youth recorded on the Eastern Front: *'Wer glücklich ist, der darf keine Furcht haben Auch nicht vor dem Tode'*? On the same day (Thursday 8 July 1916) father was writing in his *Three Years Marching with the First Brigade*: 'Our conquests were merely moral. Our losses numerous and bloody. We retreated in good order – the supplies were withdrawn intact. The trenches and the potatoes were all that was left for the Muscovites. But the Austrians were fleeing in a panic...'

In Palmer-like moments of ecstasy, clarity and tranquillity L.W.'s last words rise to my lips and I wonder whether when the time comes I will deliver for myself a similar last judgement and whether anyone will happen to hear it.

[1978]

RYSZARD KRYNICKI

Ryszard Krynicki was born in 1943 in Sankt Valentin in Austria.
He studied Polish literature at Poznań University, and has been
closely associated with the dissident movement.

Krynicki's *Organism zbiorowy (Collective organism)* which includes
translations of Austrian and German poets (most prominently
Brecht) was published in 1975. He was subsequently barred from
publication in Poland and his next volume appeared in Paris in 1978
in Institut Littéraire's 'Uncensored' series. This volume, entitled
Nasze życie rośnie (Our life flourishes) was in 1980 reprinted by a
clandestine press in Kraków.

Krynicki: 'The institutionalised, fetishistic language, the language
of newspaper slogans, which is a reflection of the general falsification
of reality – all this stands revealed, unmasked and negated. Linguis-
tic poetry speaks of the present in its own language subjected to a
poetic critique.'

Theoretical terms are fated to turn into their opposites: this has
happened to "linguistic poetry". With reference to Krynicki's work
it signifies, as he is at pains to stress, a focussing on ordinary con-
temporary speech, but the term is also employed to describe Kar-
powicz's "Mallarméan" objectivication of language.

'The principle of "blossoming poetry", which governs Krynicki's work, is simply a consequence of the sickness of social consciousness: nothing can be named univocally, falsehood hides behind every meaning...

'By holding on faithfully to Peiper's postulate about 'sewing into our man a nerve of the present', Krynicki's poetry has become the most firmly embedded in the specifics of modern life. But his embrace of the present is conducted not on the plane of co-existence of ideas or of commenting on events, but on an artistic level, that is, his poetry attempts to extract from the new, complicated and often falsified reality, new forms of beauty, it seeks to construct a certain aesthetic idea...He consciously relates to Peiper's programme of "artistic construction" which consists of "bringing order into chaos".' (Julian Kornhauser)

While acknowledging the great achievements of Tadeusz Peiper (1891-1969) as a poetic theorist, Miłosz has also cruelly (and prematurely) dismissed his poetry as 'interesting only as an example of unflinching attachment to principles'. Premature, because when a popular selection of Peiper's poetry appeared in 1978, Krzysztof Karasek, Krynicki's contemporary, introduced it as being more influential 'then even the work of more distinguished poets'. One of Peiper's theoretical principles, which he also enshrined in his poetry and which, as is clear from Kornhauser's comments, has chiefly attracted Krynicki's and Karasek's generation, is that of the 'blossoming poem' in which, according to Peiper, 'each phase contains some common centre, which nevertheless may in each phase be expressed differently'. This mode of composition is visible in Krynicki's longer poems (and indeed length must be a prerequisite here), while the short poems show an affinity with Brecht's aphoristic metaphors.

Caute*

*He left behind several dozen books, a few
copper-plates, a green coat, an eiderdown,
seven shirts and a handful of other items.*
                          Leszek Kołakowski

Cautiously you open your palm, it's
blind and dumb. Shameless, undressed. Impressed,
identified
and registered. Spinoza's friends
and those who denied him
and those who preyed on his still warm corpse
and the worms nourished on his meat
and his enemies
and the inquisitors of his day
and the clouds crossing the frontiers of his time,
are all gone and the causes of his death are no longer news,
his coat his eiderdown and shirts
don't cover anyone, there are new books in the bookshops,
exiles are in exile, palm prints
on files, sentry-posts on frontiers, nudes in magazines,
customs-men where they are accustomed, lodgers in lodgings, jurors
     in the jury-box,
typescripts in drawers, smiles on faces, blood
in veins, workmen at work, soldiers in uniform, potatoes
in bellies, citizens in the country, uniforms in stores, identity cards
in pockets, help in need, innards inside,
hands in gloves, foreigners abroad, tongue
behind teeth, prisoners in prison, meat in tins, teeth
in cement, sputniks in space, dead in graves, sun
during the day, graves in the ground, dreams at night, earth in the
     universe
(shrinking or expanding), a break in biography,
past into present, temperature in degrees, each
one in his place, life-line in a drawer, heart
in the throat, sky in clouds, any questions

can't see any, thank you

[February 1974]

* 'Cautiously', Spinoza's motto. [Ed.]

Also

Clouds freely cross frontiers
and violate the air-space of neighbouring states,
sea-waves flow
beyond the borders of territorial waters,
the Universal Declaration of the Rights of Man
does not bear comparison with specific constitutions,
constitutions are less practical
than criminal codes:

from the moment when in countries,
in which the only place you can go to
without a passport is the earth,
they resolved to protect the natural environment,
nature's fate also

appeared to be sealed

From time to time

From time to time someone burned at the stake
wise men, madmen, casual witnesses
which could mean any one of us

women who in every bed
of their accidental epoch
burned like books
because of imagined and real contacts with imagined and real demons

like books bound in our human skin

voting for, against – and refraining from voting

from time to time our bad times became worse
when proprietors of nations proclaimed things were getting better
and would get better still
the longer the speeches – the longer the queues –

those last in the queue felt ever so closely the brazen brow
of approaching time

some were dying in concentration camps
in labour camps far north
the best of their time,
they disappeared without trace,
others knew about it but couldn't believe it,
others knew about it but wouldn't believe it,
anti-fascists died at the hands of anti-fascists,
from time to time in the encyclopaedias of our best times
adjectives changed places, entries came and went,
streets changed their names, words in newspapers
came and went
concealing genocide of nations and generations,
readers opened their newspapers and shut
doors leading to the real world
the 'god' entry was shrinking, the entry 'man' sounded equivocal,
the curfew could last for years

from time to time
we killed time, we wasted life
we wasted time, we killed life
many mouldered in prisons of their accidental epochs
many times the treacherous knife of a foreign heart penetrated our hearts
banished were also
those who vainly tried to journey beyond the frontiers
of their accidental epoch

struggles for peace absorbed as many victims
as battles for control
some betrayed friends
instead of fighting the internal foe
who had conquered their hearts
from time to time
the red pencil of stupefied censorship of death
employing mostly graduates in History and Law
opened someone's bayonet-gashed face
long lost by its accidental owner and slave
in hastily closed covers of an identity-card
of an accidental association of confidential interlocutors,
of a meek association of compulsory interlocutors,

of a compulsory association of meek interlocutors,
of a private association etc. of its epoch

from time to time these identity-cards with slammed faces
burned at the stake,
kindling the bright bodies of presidential tables,
inflaming the red cloth of an inhuman world
nylon flags ran with artificial blood

from time to time our hearts and faces were like passing banners

from time to time we were on everyone's lips
everyone's lips received us or spat us out
the young fought the old, the old fought the young,
there was no chance of a balance
because the former grew older more quickly than the latter dared
    speak
and thus we outstripped the epoch
what we called luck – youth –
we had as a gift of nature and not from the state which was our
    property
some mouldered in prisons or psychiatric camps
others received decorations and high pensions
receivers of stolen goods became ambassadors
from time to time history, whose graduates most often
work in a stupefied censorship of death
agreed with some and disagreed with others
from time to time out of envy or stupidity our replete contemporaries
    denied us subsistence
from time to time they demolished statues
of the laureates of their accidental epoch
and posthumously rehabilitated the victims of laureates
of the previous epoch

from time to time Stalin's balsamed mummy
was ready to return,

from time to time professional assassins
established the death penalty,
progressive cancer of lies was consuming the epoch
which like every terminal case to the end naively believed
it was progressing under its own strength to a better future

from time to time we had no time
to try and change our times
tell the time of our only life
from various other times, in which we happened to live,
politicians, preachers, artists and poets,
we always found something to justify them,
sometimes we simply wished to survive,
when we came to believe freedom means consciousness of the
        necessity
of living in our best possible world
which is building an even better one, a better-adjusted world
and can no longer find for itself any free space, any gap
in the general happiness

Polish Press Agency

The Polish Press Agency reports
a successful hijacking of an airliner
by freedom fighters.
It demonstrated 'the total ineffectiveness
of the secret services, repression
and other tools of the blood-thirsty dictator'
– the PPA explains to its readers in our
(as it says itself) camp
in which even unproven intentions

end in death sentences.

Ad hominem

Just before the attack by the Third Reich
on the allied Soviet Union
Berthold Brecht on the run from the Nazis
stopped in the Socialist Paradise
which he had lauded so often
for only as long as circumstances demanded
and breathed freely only when

he arrived in the United States
about which he had little good

to say.

You receive letters

You receive letters with stamps
on which a country is depicted like a flag
fluttering in the wind

the white corpse of the letter folds and unfolds its hands
the white dove of the letter folds and unfolds its wings
while the wind fluttering against the banners
while the wind tangled in the banners

behaves in conformity with its nature
and changes nothing

RAFAŁ WOJACZEK

'I was born in 1945. I attended schools, I grew up in libraries, on railway stations, in other people's homes, more or less, in bars of various categories and in other places. I swam in rivers, lakes, in great waters even. I partook of Adventure – "The land was mine, alas". At times I died and then from the other side of life I would cry: bee! Enough?'

Wojaczek spent six months studying literature at Kraków University and then worked in Wrocław in a garage. In 1971 he committed suicide. His *Collected Works* appeared in 1976 with a long introductory essay by Tymoteusz Karpowicz.

'Lacking a world to accept fully or in part, Wojaczek, like many writers, decided to create his own world...As a total Romantic, terribly anachronistic in an age of computers, Wojaczek decided upon an empiricism possible only in the confined area of his organism ...The first idea concerned his own death...The next were closely tied to it, were its pseudonyms and designations: poetry and woman ...The coherence of the examined phenomena was surprisingly great and already in Wojaczek's earliest poems it was difficult to see whether his subject is poetry or death, death or love, woman or Poland.' (Tymoteusz Karpowicz)

'He was considered by his admirers the first truly worthy successor of Bursa, and some have called him "a Polish Rimbaud". Both these opinions obviously need to be qualified. However, just as there was something Rimbaudian in Wojaczek's talent: in its precociousness, intensity of vision and stylistic virtuosity, so his uncompromising frankness of expression and the savage flouting of taboos recall Bursa.

'But in contrast to Bursa's, Wojaczek's poems have a formal and stylistic finish that blunts and often alleviates their brutal impact... Their tone, despite the brutal effects, is lyrical, and sometimes sentimental, and they are frequently expressed in the form of lullabies, ballads, songs and incantations.' (Bogdan Czaykowski)

An attempted poem

A leaf of my brain droops sadly
From the branch of such hot July
    And a strange tiny insect walks
    Along the path of one of its veins

Maybe it's a cockroach or possibly a grateful
Ladybird fat with the sky's lard
    The brain knows what I don't
    When I lie beneath the tree of July

I sleep when the brain constantly tickled
By the multiplying tiny leg cannot sleep
    And when I sleep more soundly
    The brain sees the more widely

Now it sees the poem's landscape
And it hears the poem's music
    It's not afraid the way
    I surely would have been

It sees a river where a woman
Swims nakedly   Her body is a pregnant barge
    It hears the cataract
    That will wreck that barge

And it sees yet other women
Suitably naked since they took
    Off their dresses before they entered
    The poem's reach   And the Creator

Still stands and they draw matches
To establish the order of love
    And how they cheat   But he
    Modestly observes the river's

Current and chucking the wood he
Counts the seconds   But behold the gallows
    Which slowly grew behind
    His back out of the planted seed

And yet it sprouted in a different poem
A female shade fondles his nape   The Creator
    Lowers his head   The brain
    Laughs when the creative

    Masculinity rises straight to the sun's mouth
But suddenly the ladybird or
    Cockroach falls off the brain   No one knows
    Because I wake the brain sleeps

Could I in frail lips carry such love

Infinitely carefree
    somewhere at the close
      of the 24 hours
I fell asleep so, at last
    not in Your dream, but
      in mine!

– Suddenly I woke
    naked
    from sleepy embraces
of nightmarish hands – mumbling
    a dream from sleep, this
      thought: father

and God already sitting at the foot
of the bed – he held a nightdress
in his hands – mine!
    did I myself
      take it off
        in sleep ?

– I cried, covering my eyes
with a thoughtless hand:
when I removed it – the wise
      God
    was no longer
    waiting for me.

– He surely flew away
    on a cloud
  of the dress
since I did not find it
   either at the feet or
     anywhere.

– Know: biting with bloody
   gums the pen
    I write
this letter to cover up
    my nakedness
   at least with such a leaf.

[28 May 1970]

The end of poetry

The end of poetry ought to come in a dark hallway
Of a tenement block stinking of cabbages and bogs
Ought to be the unexpected blessing of a knife
Below the shoulder-blade or a crowbar in the skull like a laconic amen

For it ought to be a tank of a speeding sky
The end of poetry ought to be swifter even than thought
In order to cry what might signify rebellion or sorrow
The end of poetry ought to be ungrammatical

STANISŁAW BARAŃCZAK

Stanisław Barańczak was born in 1946 in Poznań; he studied literature at Poznań University and became a lecturer there in 1969. He has published poetry, literary criticism and translations of English metaphysical poets, Gerard Manley Hopkins, e.e. cummings and Dylan Thomas. He became closely associated with the leading dissident periodical *Zapis*. When invited to a visiting professorship at Harvard, he was initially refused permission to leave Poland but in 1981 was eventually allowed to take up his appointment. He has published in Paris a large collection of critical essays on contemporary Polish literature significantly entitled *Etyka i poetyka* and in London a study of Zbigniew Herbert's poetry.

Along with Jacek Bierezin, Krzysztof Karasek, Julian Kornhauser, Ryszard Krynicki, Ewa Lipska, Witold Sułkowski and Adam Zagajewski, Barańczak belongs to the generation which came into prominence in the late sixties. Unlike the fifties generation, which at its worst produced the baroque mannerisms of Grochowiak and the infantile chatter of Harasymowicz, this generation speaks a simpler language. Whereas previously, the poets' likely reaction to the abuse of power and official lies was to escape completely either into surrealism, neo-classicism or linguistic fireworks, the present generation boldly took on the state on its own terms. Barańczak persistently and meticulously constructs his poems out of bureaucratic paraphernalia, official communiqués and political oratory, as in 'Please complete legibly in block capitals':

> Born? (yes, no; delete if not
> applicable); why 'yes'? (give reasons); where,
> when, why, for whom do you live?
> . . .
>   Knowledge of foreign
> bodies and tongues? orders, decorations?
> special marks? the state of your courage?
> do you intend to have children? (yes, no); why
> 'no'?

As a close student of English-language poetry, Barańczak appreciates the effectiveness of ambiguity and punning, qualities only rarely explored in Polish poetry. In his poems he skilfully fuses political double-talk, intended to deceive, with a poetic exploration of the variety of meanings inherent in any verbal utterance. The result is that the mechanism of official lies is unmasked and the process itself produces an aesthetically satisfying metaphorical complexity. What will bear witness to our times? asks Barańczak and explains:

Not our history textbooks, which no one
will open, why should they, not newspapers,
which were never open
to reality (except in the case of a few
obituaries and weather forecasts), not letters,
which are so frequently opened that
there was nothing we could write openly in them,
not even literature, also shut tight
in itself, in officials' drawers or in
tiny cardboard coffins of carved up editions;
if anything remains, it will be the open eyes
of that child, which today can't understand
our closed world...

Browsing through *Homes & Gardens*

So, that's how things are in that world; but
let's show vigilance, let's not be deceived, that
furniture of theirs also gets covered with dust, those juicy
steaks tend to be overdone, those lawns have
continually to be cut, dust, ashes, the mower's
roar in that world too they
have sometimes bled, some of them
are dead, their tanned and massaged
faces also sometimes grow pale and sweat;

and moreover we too have our achievements,

our products are in the lead, our
positive appearances succeed more and
more often, our endeavours do not recede, our
youth accedes to the ranks, our visible effects
proceed when specific activities are embraced;

and yet in this world some have always bled,
even when all goes smoothly, there is someone dead,
and if he is alive, it's only in the other
world there is nothing for one to be dying,
only there everything is not for bleeding
and not for believing

These men, so powerful

These men, so powerful, always shown
a little from below by crouching cameramen, lifting
a heavy foot to crush me, no, to
mount the aircraft steps, lifting their hands
at me, no, in order to greet crowds
obediently waving flags, those signing
my death warrant, no, only a trade
agreement dried immediately with an obliging
blotter,

those so brave, with such uplifted brows
standing in open cars, so
manfully inspecting the front of harvest work, as though
when stepping into a furrow they entered a trench,
those with a hard fist, capable of thumping lecterns
and patting shoulders
of men bent in salute, just pinned
with medals to black suits,

always
you feared them so,
you were so tiny
compared to them, always standing above
you, on stairs, rostrums, tribunes,
but surely it's enough to stop being
afraid for at least one moment, let's say:
start being afraid a little less
so that you realise
it is they who are most afraid

BRONISŁAW MAJ

Bronisław Maj was born in 1953 in Łódź. He studied literature at Kraków University and published his first book of poems in 1980.

Barańczak and Krynicki belong to a generation of vocal dissidents, but in Maj's poetry the political note is muted and frequently absent altogether. Nevertheless, the fact that in 1984 Solidarity distinguished him with an honorary prize, and the fact that his latest collection *Zagłada świętego miasta (Annihilation of the Holy City)* was published in London, rather than Warsaw, stamps him as a dissident.

The first impression of Maj's poetry is one of great delicacy, gentleness and inwardness. 'My imagination is particular', he declares and proclaims his ideal poem to be 'as brief as the life of a cabbage white'. But we soon realise that we need to listen more seriously to this quiet voice which also says:

> I am a poet: I wish to know whether this means anything
> to you, whether I can help in any way.

It is, however, the poet who needs help, specifically moral advice, since:

> For years, day after day, breathing lies, we had lost
> the distinction of good and evil.

But, ultimately,

> whatever the poet talks about, he
> always talks about his freedom

And while in one poem Maj thinks he can communicate with a poet
a hundred years hence because of shared basic sense-experiences,
in another he realises there is a barrier to understanding at a deeper
level:

> We've lived here too long, breathed this
> epoch in too deeply...to say
> the truth about it

Nevertheless, a general notion about the epoch can by acquired,
since in it the poet 'lied to preserve truth' and tried to achieve
incompatible objectives: 'to survive and be clean', a particularly acute
moral dilemma for a writer in a country where the state tempts him
with rich rewards for conformity.

Maj's metaphysical longing to preserve the passing moment, his
preference for the minimal description and his concern over the
state of the Polish nation, all come together in the following poem,
which records a certain incident in Kraków in March 1980.

'This lasts barely a few minutes'

21st March, 1980, in Kraków

This lasts barely a few minutes: the largest market-place in old
Europe, a misty morning, the city's voices are still uncertain – then:
a fire, blindingly yellow, terrifies and disables them: they stop dealing
in dollars and vodka in the bank's doorways, trembling circles
of the crowd converge on a man who burns, chained to a hydrant.
        The reek of petrol,
swiftly: his clothes, then his hair, shaking hands and lips: a voice
distorted in pain is only a cry, will not
succeed as words, the dark acrid smoke of the rejected sacrifice
        doesn't rise
to heaven, will not freeze into a sign: it crawls low, vanishes
absorbed in the hungry lungs of the crowd, which – only some
minutes later – will choose life: in the doorways opposite they are
again dealing in dollars and vodka, calm circles
of the crowd disperse, the last flame of old Europe
dies away and the city's triumphal voice
sets: 'Burning, how can you tell
whether you are waxing free or
whether what is yours is doomed
to destruction.'*

'A leaf'

A leaf, one of the last, broke off a maple branch,
it swirls in clear October air, falls
on a pile of other leaves, grows dark and still. No one
admired its rousing battle with the wind,
no one followed its flight, no one will distinguish it now
lying among other leaves, no one had seen
what I had, no one. I am
alone.

* The quotation comes from Norwid's play about the early Greek poet
Tyrtaios, described in a recently published Polish reference book as 'a
symbol of national struggle'. [Ed.]

Bibliography
SOURCES OF QUOTATIONS IN THE NOTES

Lesław Bartelski, 'Prawo przyjaźni', *W gałązce dymu, w ognia blasku*, ed. Józef Szczypka (Warszawa, 1977).

Maciej Broński, 'Tryb porozumiewawczy', *Kultura* no.11-422 (November 1982), 105-109.

Andrzej Bursa, *Utwory wierszem i prozą*, ed. Stanisław Stanuch (Kraków, 1969).

Bogdan Czaykowski, 'Po okresie "burzy i naporu"', *Merkuriusz* no.4-96 (April 1958), 1-3.

Bogdan Czaykowski, 'Post-war Polish Poets', *The Tradition of Polish Ideals*, ed. W.J. Stankiewicz (London, 1981).

Jan Darowski, 'Polish Poetry Supplement', *Oficyna Poetów* no.1-16 (February 1970), 22-28.

Jan Darowski, 'Polish Poetry Supplement', *Oficyna Poetów* no.3-18 (August 1970), 20-30.

Juliusz Gomulicki, *Cyprian Norwid: Przewodnik po życiu i twórczości* (Warszawa, 1970).

Zbigniew Herbert, 'A Poet of Exact Meaning' [Interview], *PN Review* no. 26 (vol.6 no.6, 1982), 8-12.

Tomasz Jodełka-Burzecki, *Leopold Staff: Gałąź kwitnąca* (Warszawa, 1968).

Julian Kornhauser and Adam Zagajewski, *Świat nie przedstawiony* (Kraków, 1974).

Anka Kowalska, 'Poems from an Internment Camp', *Index on Censorship*, vol.12 no.2 (April 1983), 16-18.

Ryszard Krynicki, 'Czy istnieje już poezja lingwistyczna?', *Poezja* no.3-205 (1972), 47-51.

Danuta Künstler, 'Pomyśl: człowiekiem jesteś a chwalisz ciemności', *Poezja* no.3-205 (1983), 88-90.

Alicja Lisiecka, *Kto jest 'Księciem Poetów'?* (London, 1979).

Zygmunt Ławrynowicz, 'Krytyk i poeta', *Merkuriusz* no.3-83 (March 1957), 8-9

Czesław Miłosz, *The History of Polish Literature* (London, 1969).

Tadeusz Peiper, *Myśli o poezji* (Kraków, 1974).

Tadeusz Peiper, *Poezje wybrane*, ed. and intro. Krzysztof Karasek (Warszawa, 1978).

Jan Sobota, 'Wspomnienia o Wierzyńskim i Staffie', *Tygodnik Powszechny* no.10/1810 (4 March 1984), 5.

Tadeusz Sołtan, 'Pokolenie nie zmarnowane', *op.cit.* ed. Józef Szczypka (Warszawa, 1977).

Rafał Wojaczek, *Utwory zebrane*, intro. Tymoteusz Karpowicz (Wrocław, 1976).

Further reading
BOOKS BY POETS FROM THIS ANTHOLOGY

Zbigniew Herbert, *Report from the Besieged City and other poems*, trs. John and Bogdana Carpenter (Oxford University Press, 1987).

Zbigniew Herbert, *Selected Poems*, trs. Czesław Miłosz and Peter Dale Scott (Penguin, 1969; reissued by Carcanet, 1987).

Zbigniew Herbert, *Selected Poems*, trs. John and Bogdana Carpenter (Oxford University Press, 1977).

Ryszard Krynicki, *Citizen R.K. does not live*, trs. R.A. Davies and J.M. Gogol (Forest Grove, 1985).

Cyprian Kamil Norwid, *Poezje/Poems*, trs. Adam Czerniawski (Wydawnictwo Literackie, Kraków, 1986).

Tadeusz Różewicz, *Conversation with the Prince and other poems*, trs. Adam Czerniawski (Anvil Press Poetry, 1982).

Tadeusz Różewicz, *Faces of Anxiety*, trs. Adam Czerniawski (Rapp & Whiting, 1969).

Tadeusz Różewicz, *Green Rose*, trs. Geoffrey Thurley (John Michael Group, Darlington, Australia, 1982).

Tadeusz Różewicz, *Selected Poems*, trs. Adam Czerniawski (Penguin, 1976).

Tadeusz Różewicz, *The Survivor and other poems*, trs. M.J. Krynski and R.A. Maguire (Princeton University Press, 1976).

Tadeusz Różewicz, *Unease*, trs. Victor Contoski (New Rivers Press, Minnesota, 1980).

Leopold Staff, *An Empty Room*, trs. Adam Czerniawski (Bloodaxe Books, 1983).

Leon Zdzisław Stroiński, *Window*, trs. Adam Czerniawski (Oasis Books, 1979).

Wisława Szymborska, *Sounds, Feelings, Thoughts: Seventy Poems*, trs. M.J. Krynski and R.A. Maguire (Princeton University Press, 1981).

BLOODAXE BOOKS

INTERNATIONAL WRITING

IRINA RATUSHINSKAYA
No, I'm Not Afraid
Translated by David McDuff

Why was a 28-year-old woman sentenced to seven years' hard labour
for writing these poems?
'She is a remarkably genuine poet, a poet with faultless pitch...
natural, with a voice of her own, piercing but devoid of hysteria'
— JOSEPH BRODSKY

TOMAS TRANSTRÖMER
Collected Poems
Translated by Robin Fulton

'Robin Fulton's translation from the Swedish is excellent: a poet of
exceptional achievement has with this volume been born into
English — GUARDIAN

MARINA TSVETAYEVA
Selected Poems
Translated by David McDuff

This important new translation makes available complete versions of
Tsvetayeva's major long poems and poem cycles: *Poem of the End,
An Attempt at a Room, Poems to Czechia* and *New Year Letter.*
David McDuff's edition is based on the new definitive Russica text
of Tsvetayeva's poetry.

MIROSLAV HOLUB
The Fly

Poems by the Young Holub, including the classic work of his Penguin
Selected Poems. Translations by George Theiner, Ewald Osers, and
Ian and Jarmila Milner. 'One of the sanest voices of our time'
— A. ALVAREZ

MIROSLAV HOLUB
On the Contrary and Other Poems
Translated by Ewald Osers

Miroslav Holub is Czechoslovakia's most important poet, and also
one of her leading scientists. This book presents a decade of new
work. 'One of the half dozen most important poets writing anywhere'
— TED HUGHES.

INTERNATIONAL WRITING

MARIN SORESCU
Selected Poems
Translated by Michael Hamburger

'Sorescu is already being tipped as a future Nobel prizewinner. His poems, however, have crowned him with the only distinction that matters. If you don't read any other new book of poetry this year, read this one' – SUNDAY TIMES

MARIN SORESCU
The Biggest Egg in the World

New poems by Romania's comic genius in versions by Seamus Heaney, Ted Hughes, David Constantine, D.J. Enright, Michael Hamburger, Michael Longley, Paul Muldoon, William Scammell, with Ioana Russell-Gebbett.

HART CRANE
Complete Poems

One of America's most important poets. Lowell called Crane 'the Shelley of my age' and 'the great poet of that generation'. This new *Complete Poems*, based on Brom Weber's definitive 1966 edition, has 22 additional poems. *Sunday Times* Paperback of the Year.

DENISE LEVERTOV
Selected Poems

'She is the most subtly skilful poet of her generation, the most profound, the most modest, the most moving' – NEW YORK TIMES This new *Selected Poems* covers all Denise Levertov's collections up to *Candles in Babylon*.

DENISE LEVERTOV
Oblique Prayers

In America this new book was seen as marking a new phase in Levertov's work – more meditative yet still firmly rooted in everyday experience. It includes her translations of 14 poems by the contemporary French poet Jean Joubert.

LEOPOLD STAFF
An Empty Room
Translated by Adam Czerniawski

'Staff's poetry, which is widely admired in Poland, is mischievously and amiably laconic...It is a delightful book, the sort you put down wishing there was more, full of teasing wit, sly humour, clear observation and simplicity of style' – DOUGLAS DUNN

POETRY WITH AN EDGE

JENI COUZYN (editor)
Bloodaxe Book of Contemporary Women Poets
Large selections – with essays on their work – by eleven leading
British poets: Sylvia Plath, Stevie Smith, Kathleen Raine, Fleur
Adcock, Anne Stevenson, Elaine Feinstein, Elizabeth Jennings,
Jenny Joseph, Denise Levertov, Ruth Fainlight and Jeni Couzyn.
Illustrated with photographs of the writers.

R.S. THOMAS
Selected Poems 1946-1968
R.S. Thomas is one of the most important poets of our time. This is
his own selection from six of the finest books of poetry published
since the war. 'One of the half-dozen best poets now writing in English
...His example reduces most modern verse to footling whimsy'
– KINGSLEY AMIS

FRANCES HOROVITZ
Collected Poems
'She has perfect rhythm, great delicacy and a rather Chinese yet very
locally British sense of landscape...her poetry does seem to me to
approach greatness' – PETER LEVI

STEWART CONN
In the Kibble Palace
Stewart Conn is one of Scotland's finest poets. As well as new poems,
this book draws upon five previous collections, including *Stoats in
the Sunlight* (1968) and *Under the Ice* (1978), winners of Scottish Arts
Council Awards, and *An Ear to the Ground* (1972), a Poetry Book
Society Choice.

ARTHUR GIBSON
Boundless Function
A totally new kind of literature: but is it autobiography, philosophy
or poetry? Frank Kermode claims this book is so different from
anything else that it creates a new *genre*. Poet and philosopher
Arthur Gibson has been called 'the last Renaissance man' and
'a madman or a genius'.

KATHLEEN JAMIE
The Way We Live
'She can make unrhetorical language glow with mystery. It is seldom
that one reads a gifted poet whose work stands aside from the
currents of the day...Kathleen Jamie writes so convincingly already
that one's duty is just to read her poems' – PETER PORTER, *Observer*

POETRY BOOK SOCIETY
RECOMMENDATIONS

KEN SMITH
Wormwood
Poems from Smith's two-year stint as writer-in-residence at
Wormwood Scrubs prison. 'He opens up hidden layers of common
fear, suffering and desire' – CHICAGO SUN-TIMES

KEN SMITH
Terra
'Ken Smith is probably the most important poet writing today, one of
the very few who will still be read a hundred years from now as a
man whose vision encompassed and explained his times – TRIBUNE

MARTIN STOKES
The First Death of Venice
Enigmatic, unusual, highly skilful and totally original, this first
collection will establish Stokes as a remarkable new voice in
contemporary British poetry.

JOHN HARTLEY WILLIAMS
Bright River Yonder
A baroque Wild West poetry adventure by the winner of the Arvon
Poetry Competition. Indescribable and utterly compelling.

DAVID CONSTANTINE
Madder
Constantine won the Alice Hunt Bartlett Prize in 1984, and with it
the judges' praise for 'a generous, self-aware sensuality which he can
express in a dazzling variety of tones on a wide range of themes.'

PETER DIDSBURY
The Classical Farm
'Peter Didsbury is a clever and original poet…He can be
simultaneously knowing and naive, wittily deflationary yet alive to
every leap of the post-Romantic eye…a soaring, playful imagination
…I suspect that he is the best new poet that the excellent Bloodaxe
Books have yet published' – William Scammell, TLS

JAMES SIMMONS
Poems 1956 -1986
Irish poet and singer James Simmons has been much praised for his
'atrocious honesty' (*Irish Times*), for being 'a dangerous truth-teller'
(*Guardian*), 'humane, entertaining, honest' (*TLS*) and 'tender,
sensual, totally unromantic and totally honest' (Adrian Henri). This
new, large selection includes poems from nine previous books,
including *Judy Garland and the Cold War*, *Constantly Singing*, and
From the Irish.

AUTHORS PUBLISHED BY

BLOODAXE BOOKS

FLEUR ADCOCK	DOUGLAS HOUSTON
BASIL BUNTING	PAUL HYLAND
ANGELA CARTER	KATHLEEN JAMIE
JOHN CASSIDY	B.S. JOHNSON
SID CHAPLIN	JENNY JOSEPH
EILÉAN NÍ CHUILLEANÁIN	BRENDAN KENNELLY
STEWART CONN	SIRKKA-LIISA KONTTINEN
DAVID CONSTANTINE	DENISE LEVERTOV
JENI COUZYN	EDNA LONGLEY
HART CRANE	SHENA MACKAY
ADAM CZERNIAWSKI	SEAN O'BRIEN
PETER DIDSBURY	JOHN OLDHAM
JOHN DREW	TOM PAULIN
HELEN DUNMORE	IRINA RATUSHINSKAYA
DOUGLAS DUNN	CAROL RUMENS
STEPHEN DUNSTAN	DAVID SCOTT
G.F. DUTTON	JAMES SIMMONS
LAURIS EDMOND	MATT SIMPSON
STEVE ELLIS	KEN SMITH
RUTH FAINLIGHT	EDITH SÖDERGRAN
EVA FIGES	MARIN SORESCU
TONY FLYNN	LEOPOLD STAFF
JIMMY FORSYTH	MARTIN STOKES
ARTHUR GIBSON	R.S. THOMAS
PAMELA GILLILAN	TOMAS TRANSTRÖMER
ANDREW GREIG	MARINA TSVETAYEVA
TONY HARRISON	ALAN WEARNE
MIROSLAV HOLUB	NIGEL WELLS
FRANCES HOROVITZ	JOHN HARTLEY WILLIAMS

*For a complete list of poetry, fiction, drama and photography books
published by Bloodaxe, please write to:*
**Bloodaxe Books Ltd, P.O. Box 1SN,
Newcastle upon Tyne NE99 1SN.**